MOUNTAIN BIKING

IN WEST VIRGINIA

MOUNTAIN BIKING IN WEST VIRGINIA

by Frank Hutchins

QUARRIER PRESS
Charleston, WV 25301

Quarrier Press
118 Capitol Street
Charleston, WV 25301
©1995 by Frank Hutchins

Book, cover and map design:
Mark Phillips/Marketing+Design Group

First edition

Printed in the United States of America on recycled paper.

Library of Congress Catalog Card Number: 95-69785

Dedicated to my parents,
"Sonny" and June Hutchins

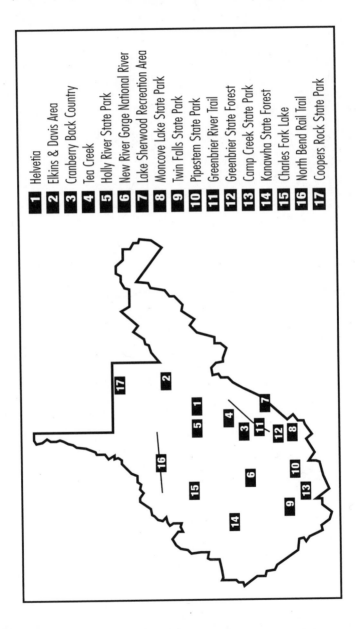

1 Helvetia
2 Elkins & Davis Area
3 Cranberry Back Country
4 Tea Creek
5 Holly River State Park
6 New River Gorge National River
7 Lake Sherwood Recreation Area
8 Moncove Lake State Park
9 Twin Falls State Park
10 Pipestem State Park
11 Greenbrier River Trail
12 Greenbrier State Forest
13 Camp Creek State Park
14 Kanawha State Forest
15 Charles Fork Lake
16 North Bend Rail Trail
17 Coopers Rock State Park

Contents

FOREWORD

The roads and trails of West Virginia offer today's bicyclists some of the most beautiful riding on the East Coast. Few states can match the miles of uninhabited public roads, forests, and parks offered by West Virginia. Tempting to both on- and off-road cyclists, the mountains of West Virginia are "just what the doctor ordered" for the mountain bike enthusiast. While beautiful flats and rolling hills are available for the novice mountain biker, tremendous uphills and rewarding descents will hold the attention of the more experienced rider.

The West Virginia Division of Tourism recognizes the potential for biking in West Virginia, and promotes both on- and off-road bicycling. Again, the off-road bicycling options in West Virginia surpass those of most states. This owes not only to the state's scenic beauty and topography, but also to the fact that the huge majority of trails in West Virginia's vast public lands are open to mountain bikes, unless otherwise posted. You will find some of the most beautiful and challenging rides in West Virginia in our State Parks and Forests, and in the Monongahela National Forest. Because of our resources, West Virginia is seeing more and more out-of-state mountain bikers. With the release of *Mountain Biking in West Virginia*, we hope more mountain bikers from within our state, and from without, will explore and enjoy our trails, parks, and forests.

West Virginia is also gaining recognition for its road biking opportunities. This is largely due to the exposure we receive from hosting the international road race, *The Kmart Classic of West Virginia*. With its $75,000 prize list, *The Kmart Classic* annually draws over 100 racers from around the world to participate in this highly competitive and prestigious stage race. These racers compete in, or race to, six different West Virginia cities in six days in late May, racing as much as 130 miles in a day, and averaging speeds over 25 miles per hour. The same roads that lend themselves to *The Kmart Classic* are readily available to the individual looking for a challenging but beautiful ride in West Virginia.

As with road biking, mountain biking in the state continues to grow. With the help of The West Virginia International Mountain Bike Association (WVIMBA), the state is working hard to clear and maintain new and existing trails, as well as keep existing trails open. The Division of Tourism is working to promote mountain biking opportunities, while also trying to prevent multiple use issues from arising and resulting in the closing of trails. Remember, when bicycling in West Virginia, always wear your helmet and follow the International Mountain Bicycle Association's (IMBA) "Rules of the Trail"; which generally emphasize showing respect to all other trail users.

With West Virginia's natural resources, the perseverance and financial support of the state, and the cooperation of courteous mountain bikers, the potential for the growth of mountain biking in our state is endless. *Mountain Biking in West Virginia* will increase the fun and excitement you'll experience as you explore the trails and secrets of the Mountain State. The more time you spend riding, the more West Virginia will reward you with its beauty, surprises, and adventures.

Happy Trails,

Greg Cook
Bicycle and Trails Coordinator
Division of Tourism

ACKNOWLEDGEMENTS

A number of people offered useful advice, assistance, trail information and support as I pedaled my way over and around the West Virginia hills and worked on this book. I'd like to thank several people in particular for their various contributions: Tom Hindman and John McCoy of the *Charleston Daily Mail*; Ken Batty of the National Weather Service office in Charleston; Greg Cook with the State Division of Tourism; Joe Robles with the U.S. Forest Service; Rogers McAvoy and Eleanor Mailloux of Helvetia; Roy Blankenship and Sissie Feller at Twin Falls; the people at ACE Outdoors in Minden; Robin and Paul Broughton of Mountain State Bicycles; Laird Knight; Steve Payne; Mark Phillips; and Stan Cohen.

LIST OF ABBREVIATIONS

FR — Forest Route
Hwy. — Highway
I — Interstate
Rd. — Road
Rt. — Route
Topo Quad(s) — Topographical Maps
U.S. — United States Highway
VA — Virginia Highway
WV — West Virginia Highway

INTRODUCTION

Bicycling in the Mountain State

Maps and Map Sources

Equipment

Rules of the Trail

Weather and Safety Precautions

Hunting Seasons

How to Use This Book

BICYCLING IN THE MOUNTAIN STATE

Taking on the mountains of West Virginia with two wheels and a water bottle invites challenge. West Virginia has an extensive trail system, with routes varying from tame to wild. The present network of routes is constantly being upgraded. You'll find lots of clear and casual trails, but there are still plenty of trails that are raw and unworked. The latter give bicyclists a chance to explore new territory and tame trails that slither off to who knows where. But they can also mean butt-bruising adventures over unending rocks and roots; exhausting struggles with briars and brush; and even getting lost on occasion. Don't let these prospects scare you off. Again, this book contains descriptions of all types of trails located throughout the state: easy and difficult routes; up and down and level trails; and loops and out-and-backs. The variety of rides will meet virtually anyone's needs. Both the novice and the pro will find rides they'll enjoy.

The book includes only public-access routes. While there are a vast number of trails on these public properties — some 600 miles in the Monongahela National Forest alone — there are countless trails on private property. Large coal and timber companies own much of the best biking land. Each company has its own policy for biking and hiking access. If you want to know about access on some of these properties, I suggest asking the superintendent at the nearest public park. While they might not be able to give you the OK to ride, they should be able to give you a name and number to call for such permission.

Generally, each trail description in this guide provides basic information: location, directions, length, difficulty, scenery, topo quads, estimated elevations, and highlights about the ride. I've also included some geographical and historical information, such as a brief geologic and cultural history of the New River Gorge, or the abbreviated story behind the unusual flora of the Cranberry Glades.

If you have never biked the longer and higher-elevation trails of West Virginia, do your homework before taking on such challenges. This book can help you navigate the ridges, but it can't give you more time until sundown after you've taken a wrong turn, and you can't wring water from it if your bottles are dry. Don't tackle unfamiliar trails without sufficient daylight to recover from minor mistakes. Calculate the amount of water you'll need, and take more. Pack high-energy snacks, proper tools and a well-stocked patch kit. Rain gear and a compass come in handy, too.

And take your camera. In the mountains and along the streams of West Virginia, you will find breathtaking scenery. There are incredible views, such as the cavernous New River Gorge from the Kaymoor Trail; or expansive Lake Moomaw as seen from the Allegheny Mountain Trail; and the rest of the world as you look out from Bickle Knob or Olson Tower. Each scene undergoes extraordinary changes from season to season.

You'll also find unexpected treats. By entering some of the more remote pockets of the state, you'll likely encounter wildlife usually not seen from a car window. I saw a bear and three cubs trotting about the Cranberry back country; a turkey and her poults pecking through the underbrush around Charles Fork Lake; and dozens of deer, quail, and grouse on trails all over the state.

Biking in West Virginia isn't necessarily simply a matter of pedaling from one point to another. Instead, it can be a mosaic of experiences, limited only by your imagination. This book can help get you to and through some wonderful trails, but it is by no means comprehensive. Check with local bike shops, the Monongahela National Forest ranger stations, the West Virginia Division of Tourism, and local chambers of commerce for more information. There are some trail systems I haven't included, but which offer good riding. Go out and explore!

MAPS AND MAP SOURCES

This book is a quick reference guide that can — and should — be supplemented with other information. In addition to the maps in this book, I suggest state maps, national forest maps, topography maps, field guides, and historical and cultural literature, all of which will enhance any bike trip. The following is a collection of information to help you find the trails, equip yourself for a ride, and enjoy the multitude of mountain biking experiences available in West Virginia.

Most trails in West Virginia will show up on at least one map. A state map is good for getting around on the highways, but is no help in finding specific trails and back roads. Topography maps are especially useful on the longer rides in the mountains. But remember that most topo maps for West Virginia are 20-30 years old, and many existing features won't show up on the older maps.

When biking in the Monongahela National Forest, it's useful to have a copy of the forest map put out by the National Forest Service. These maps can be purchased for around $3 in book stores and forest service offices. Call the forest service headquarters in Elkins (304) 636-1800 for more information. The state of West Virginia has recently published the *West Virginia Trails Map* and *West Virginia Cycling Guide*. These two, plus a state map, trail maps, specific state park and forest information, and other tourist information can all be obtained by calling 1-800-CALL-WVA.

In national parks and forests, trail maps may be picked up at ranger stations and visitor's centers. If you'd like to receive trail maps and general information before your visit to a national park or forest, see the addresses and phone numbers listed in Appendix 5.

EQUIPMENT

You will find a wide variety of gadgets and gizmos on the shelves of most bike shops. Some are essential; some are just fun to have. The first critical item for the bike is a small tool kit. The basic bicycle tool kit should include: wrenches (a small, adjustable wrench, a three-way wrench, and a set of Allen wrenches); a small flathead and a Phillips head screwdriver; tube repair material; tire levers; and a spare tube. A frame pump and 2 water bottle cages are mandatory. Small pouches that attach to the seat stem are useful for carrying tools. Toe clips or clipless pedals can help maximize energy use.

For the body, a helmet is a must. Many consider gloves and biking shoes indispensable, but I don't use them. Padded bike shorts are helpful for cushioning the ride. Clothing should be lightweight in hot weather, and layered for cold weather. The newer, high-tech, wicking clothes are great if you want to make the investment. I usually carry a small backpack on longer trips in which I carry food (fruit, nuts, and granola bars); a camera; a Swiss Army knife; waterproof matches; a compass; useful maps; a little money; and lightweight rain gear. Your local bike shop is the best source for additional tips on equipment.

RULES OF THE TRAIL

It is important to treat our trails with respect. We should not take trail access for granted. Cooperation between all users — bikers, hikers, equestrians, and campers — is critical. The following six rules from the International Mountain Bike Association should always be followed:

1. **Ride on open trails only.** Remember that federal and state wilderness areas are closed to bikers.
2. **Control your bicycle.** Pay attention to the trail. Obey all speed laws and traffic regulations when appropriate.
3. **Always yield the trail.** Make your approach known. A friendly hello usually works. Show

respect when passing others by slowing to a walk
or even stopping. Be prepared for others around
the next bend.

4. **Never spook animals.** All animals are startled by
sudden movements. Give animals extra room and
time to adjust to your presence. Remember that
running cattle or livestock is a serious offense.
Leave gates as you find them or as they are
marked.

5. **Plan ahead.** Know your equipment, your ability,
and your trail area. Be self-sufficient and always
wear a helmet. Keep your bike in good condition
and be equipped for changes in weather, flat tires,
etc. A well-planned trip will be more fun for you
and not a burden to others.

Below you will find paraphrased versions of the
General Rules Governing Public Use of West Virginia
State Parks that relate to mountain bike riding. While
these rules specifically apply to the state parks and forests,
it would be wise to adhere to them on all rides:

1. **It is unlawful to cut or deface any tree, rock,
or object in a state park or forest.**
2. **It is unlawful to remove any man-made or
natural object from a state park or forest.**
3. **Fires may be lit only in fireplaces or
designated areas.**
4. **Garbage may not be dumped within any state
park or forest.**
5. **Only registered campers or licensed hunters
and fishermen are authorized on the premises**

between 10:00 P.M. and 6:00 A.M.
6. Bicycles may be operated only on public roads and trails, in accordance with posted signs.
7. Use of alcoholic beverages is prohibited on all trails.

WEATHER AND SAFETY PRECAUTIONS

West Virginia weather has multiple personalities, not all of which are friendly. Mountain ranges snag storm systems as they attempt to cross the state, suddenly wringing torrents of water from the clouds. Since the weather patterns generally move west to east, the western slopes and valleys have high annual precipitation, while the eastern slopes are usually much drier. Storms can move in and throw tantrums on mountain tops, but leave valleys below virtually untouched. Some areas in the higher elevations — the Canaan Valley, along Shavers Fork, and Spruce Knob — have seen freezing temperatures in every month of the year. Fog can move in, especially between June and September, and throw a thick curtain across your path. Arctic air can sweep in from the north and plunge parts of the state into a deep freeze. All these weather features suggest that a wise biker pay close attention to the most current local forecast, and then prepare for the potential of bad weather.

Ken Batty, of the National Weather Service in Charleston, says that May and October are usually the best months for outdoor activities in West Virginia. These months usually have the calmest, driest weather — between the winter and summer storms. Batty suggests that in order to get the most localized and current weather information, use the National Weather Service's Weather Radio, which can be tuned in around the 162.4 mark on the dial of a VHF frequency radio. Small weather radios can be bought for around $20 at places such as Radio Shack. Forecasts are available 24 hours a day for a number of locations around the state. State-wide weather information can also be obtained by calling (304) 342-7771 between 8 a.m. and 4 p.m. during the week.

Following are some National Weather Service tips for weather-related hazards:

Flash Floods: During heavy rains, avoid areas subject to flooding, such as dips, low spots, canyons, and washes. Do not attempt to cross flowing streams. Do not camp along streams and washes during threatening conditions. **Lightning:** Most deaths due to lightning occur in the summer months, during the afternoon and early evening. To estimate the distance in miles between you and the lightning flash, count the seconds between the lightning and the thunder and divide by five. If you can hear thunder, you are close enough to the storm to be struck by lightning. If no sturdy shelter or car is nearby, find a low spot — away from trees, fences, and poles — that is not subject to flooding. If you are in the woods, take shelter under the shortest trees. If you feel your skin tingle or your hair stand on end, squat low to the ground on the balls of your feet. Place your hands on your knees with your head between them. Make yourself the smallest target possible, and minimize your contact with the ground.

Winter Storms: If caught in a winter storm while biking, try to find shelter, stay dry, and cover all exposed parts of the body. If shelter is not readily available, build a lean-to, wind break, or snow cave for protection from the wind. Build a fire: it will supply heat and attract attention. Place rocks around the fire to absorb and reflect the heat. Melt snow before drinking it, or it will lower your body temperature.

Heat and Sun: Cyclists should carry two water bottles and drink plenty of liquids at regular intervals to avoid dehydration. Heat exhaustion and heat stroke are always possible during the warmer months. Heat exhaustion is characterized by cool, moist, pale or flushed skin; heavy sweating; headache; nausea or vomiting; dizziness; and exhaustion. Heat stroke is characterized by hot, red skin; changes in consciousness; rapid, weak pulse; and rapid, shallow breathing. Body temperature can be very high. In either situation, get the victim to a cooler place. With heat exhaustion, remove or loosen tight clothing, and apply cool, wet cloths if available. Give the person cool water to drink, and see that they drink slowly — about half a glass every 15 minutes. Heat stroke is much more serious, even life-threatening. With a case of heat stroke, get help right away. Quickly cool the body by immersing the victim in cool water. Keep the person lying down and as cool as possible. If the victim is vomiting or losing consciousness, do not give him anything to drink.

Weather becomes a critical issue when out on a bike in the middle of nowhere. Because of a number of possibilities, (among them unpredictable weather, injuries, and bike trouble) it's best not to bike alone. However, if you prefer solitary rides, ride trails you are familiar with, let someone know where you plan to bike, and check in with them when you return.

For a chart giving the average monthly temperatures and precipitation for specific regions in the state, see Appendix 6.

Hunting Seasons

Biking amid a horde of hunters is obviously hazardous. Many state parks and forests are open to hunters, as is most of the Monongahela National Forest. If you are biking during the primary hunting seasons — deer and turkey — wear neon or brightly colored clothing; respect others in the woods; use common sense and an eagle eye. Currently hunting is not allowed on Sundays in West Virginia, making Sundays a great day to ride. Following are the hunting seasons in West Virginia:

Small Game Season: First Saturday in October through December 31.

Deer Season (rifle): Monday before Thanksgiving for two weeks.

Spring Gobbler Season: The third week in April through the third week in May.

Touring Companies

If you aren't eager to hit the mountains on your own, there are many excellent touring companies around the state. Most of these companies have experienced guides, and offer trips of varying duration and difficulty. You can go out for a few hours or a few days, and be pampered as little or as much as you like. For a list of touring companies operating in West Virginia, see Appendix 1.

HOW TO USE THIS BOOK

This guide is divided into 5 large geographic parts, which are in turn divided into chapters. Each chapter covers an area that has one or more trails. Each chapter contains a map, which shows all the trails and other pertinent information. A summary of each trail is given, which contains directions, length, and the degrees of difficulty and of interesting scenery. The rating system is not scientific; it is based on the subjective judgment of the author. Still, the ratings should give you a good idea of what to expect on each particular trail. Both the degree of difficulty and of scenery are rated on a 5-star scale. The lower the number of stars, the less difficult or the less scenic. When rating a trail on difficulty, I considered distance; degree and length of inclines; and technical challenges, such as rocks, roots and turns. A one-star trail can be ridden by beginning bikers. These are generally shorter rail trails, and other level, non-technical trails. Two-star trails can also be ridden by beginners who have a decent amount of stamina. Three-star trails are for bikers who have developed endurance and confidence in riding over obstacles and on unpredictable surfaces. Four-star trails are for experienced bikers who are looking for a good challenge. These trails are usually longer (more than

five miles), steeper, and more demanding technically. Five-star trails are few and fierce, and should be attempted only by those who are suicidal, or experienced enough to handle sharp turns, precipitous drops, and unforgiving terrain.

In addition to trail information, this book also contains suggestions on where to stay and other points of interest. It is designed to offer options, and is by no means comprehensive. For the most accurate and up-to-date information, check with the state through the toll-free tourism number, 1-800-CALL-WVA. Also check with touring centers and bike shops. (*See* Appendices 1 and 4.) West Virginia is full of the unexpected, so be flexible and adventurous. A biking trip in the Mountain State can be just that, or it can be a full-blown excursion in which you experience the culture and natural beauty of some truly out-of-the-way places.

DISCLAIMER

Neither the author nor the publisher assumes any liability for accidents happening to, or injuries sustained by, readers who engage in the activities described in this book.

POTOMAC HIGHLANDS

1. HELVETIA

I explored the back roads around Helvetia because it's my favorite spot in West Virginia. I was also pretty sure it would offer some excellent riding, and it did. I chose mainly the deserted gravel roads that wind through the mountains around this lovely community, offering beautiful views of one of the state's more remote areas.

Swiss immigrants settled Helvetia and several surrounding communities in the 1800's. Evidence of their heritage is everywhere. Home and barn construction, food, music, and other customs still bear the marks of the early Swiss, giving the area a special charm and unique character. This precious pocket is reached by navigating worn threads of asphalt known as Randolph County roadways. Nature, however, is much more generous than the local road department. Deer and turkey are plentiful here; wildflowers dot the roadsides and pastures; rhododendrons, hemlocks, and maples cover the mountains; and dancing streams churn down the hillsides.

A bike trip to Helvetia can be planned to coincide with one of the area's annual festivals, which are listed at the end of this chapter. You can also tie it in with a trip to Holly River State Park or Kumbrabow State Forest. Both are nearby and have bike trails.

Directions: From Charleston, take I-79 North to the Flatwoods exit. Next take WV 4/U.S. 19 North through

Ireland. Follow WV 4 into Rock Cave, where the road joins WV 20. Go left past Rock Cave and the West Virginia Wildlife Center. Then take a right, and follow Rt. 46 through Alexander and Czar, then into Helvetia. This winding trip on Rt. 46 should take 30-40 minutes.

From the north, take I-79 South. Next take the Buckhannon exit at Rt. 33. In Buckhannon, follow the signs for WV 20 south and the Wildlife Center. Take a left at the Wildlife Center, then follow Rt. 46 into Helvetia.

HELVETIA - SELBYVILLE - CZAR:
Location: Randolph County.
Length: 13 mile loop.
Degree of Difficulty: ***
Scenery: ****
Topo Quads: Pickens and Alton.
Elevations (in feet): Helvetia, 2,239; Selbyville, 1,886; Czar, 2,175.
Footnotes: This is an easy ride for anyone with decent stamina, and it's a great way to see the local countryside.

Description: This loop begins on the gravel road between the Hutte Restaurant and the Beekeeper Inn in Helvetia. The road travels beside a creek, then rises slightly and passes the local cemetery. Stop and check out the headstones of the early settlers. Next make a climb of about 1 mile. At the mountain top you begin a series of descents that take you through hemlock and maple forests and past small farms. At 3.4 miles, stop for the view on your left of a mountain stream as it rushes downhill toward the road, then hurries back into the woods. At 4.8 miles, you reach Selbyville, a community of several houses and a post office. Follow the main road as it curves to the right. At 5.5 miles there is a stop sign and an intersection with a paved road. Take a right and cross the bridge. Stay right after you cross the bridge on Buckhannon River Rd. (11/20). Here the road turns to gravel again.

As you leave Selbyville, there is an old schoolhouse on your left, where first through eighth grades were once taught. The road from here to Czar is level and pleasant, taking you through mostly woods. At 8.4 miles you have to wade the Buckhannon River, which can be cold even in summer. This should not be a problem, as the water didn't even reach my knees. (You can check the level in advance by driving in from Czar on the other side.) After crossing the river you have a shady, 2 mile stretch that takes you to the paved road at Czar. Take a right here for an easy ride back to Helvetia, just under 3 miles away. The total ride is about 13 miles.

HELVETIA CEMETERY LOOP:
Location: Randolph County.
Length: 3 miles.
Degree of Difficulty: ***
Scenery: ***
Topo Quad: Pickens.
Elevations (in feet): Helvetia, 2,239; at switchback, 2,570.
Footnotes: This short ride is a good way to get warmed up for a longer trip while seeing some mountain scenery.

Description: This route begins in Helvetia on the same gravel road between the Beekeeper Inn and the Hutte Restaurant (see first route above). Go past the cemetery. At 1.2 miles, take a left at a sharp switchback. From the turn, you'll pedal uphill a bit, then reach the ridge. At 1.9 miles there is a fork; stay left and begin the descent. Be careful — the slope is rutted and rocky, and you can easily be thrown. At 2.7 miles you'll intersect with another gravel road. Be careful here. There is a deep ditch as one road meets the other, and if you hit it with any speed you'll be eating gravel. Take a left here, and another left on the paved road at the bottom of the hill. You're back in Helvetia after a total ride of 3 miles.

PICKENS - SELBYVILLE
(WITH ALTERNATE ROUTES TO HELVETIA OR SILICA):
Location: Randolph County.
Length: 10-15 miles, depending on route chosen.
Degree of Difficulty: Varies, but generally ***
Scenery: ****
Topo Quads: Pickens; and Alton (for Selbyville option).
Elevations (in feet): Pickens, 2,700; main intersection, 2,918; Silica, 2,350; Selbyville, 1,886.
Footnotes: The options here offer a sampling of high mountain country in one of the state's most isolated regions. Pickens is an old timber and rail town that once boomed with its own opera house, banks and hotels. It now is a shadow of the boomtown, but is still worth a look around. You'll find a museum here with lots of local history, and a couple of annual festivals that draw large crowds. You can also ask a local to point out the grave of

George the Leper, a Lebanese immigrant. He was sent to Pickens by the rail company he worked for when they discovered he had leprosy. He lived in a tent here, was fed by a local family, and cared for by a local doctor. A small grave surrounded by a rail fence marks the spot where he was buried.

Description: It's best to have someone shuttle you to Pickens on Rt. 45 to start this ride, unless you want to bike the 5 miles on the hilly, paved road from Helvetia. The gravel road beside Been's Store, Rt. 50, is a good place to start a foray into the surrounding hills. This road can take you several places: to Selbyville, back to Helvetia, or to Silica. Silica is a ghost town that once housed workers who mined silica for export to international markets.

About 1.7 miles down Rt. 50, you'll climb until reaching the 2.5 mile mark. At the 3 mile mark is an intersection. Here you determine which town you're going to. A right takes you back to Helvetia, over 2 miles away with steep climbs. On the road to Helvetia you'll find a grassy knob that offers a great overlook of the surrounding mountains. A left at the intersection takes you downhill to Silica. The ride down to Silica is steep, meaning the ride back up is hard. Going straight at the intersection, you stay on Rt. 50 to reach Selbyville. Heading down Rt. 50, at the 6.3 mile mark you'll reach the road that passes the Helvetia cemetery. You can take a right here for a ride of several miles back to Helvetia, or a left to go to Selbyville. From Selbyville you can turn around and retrace your path, or go right and through Czar as described in the Helvetia-Selbyville-Czar loop.

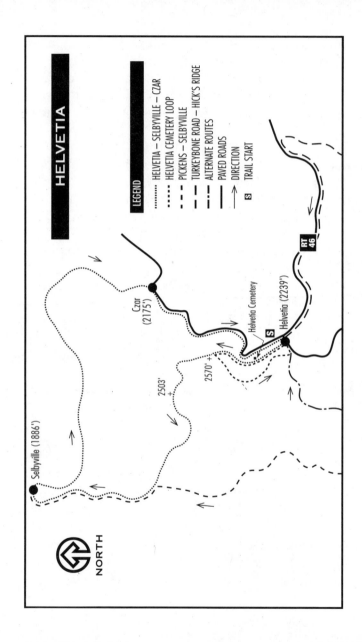

HELVETIA

LEGEND

········· HELVETIA – SELBYVILLE – CZAR
∙∙∙∙∙∙∙∙∙ HELVETIA CEMETERY LOOP
– – – – PICKENS – SELBYVILLE
———— TURKEYBONE ROAD – HICK'S RIDGE
–∙–∙– ALTERNATE ROUTES
———— PAVED ROADS
→ DIRECTION
S TRAIL START

Selbyville (1886')

2503'
+

2570'+

Czar
(2175')

Helvetia Cemetery

S

Helvetia (2239')

RT
46

NORTH

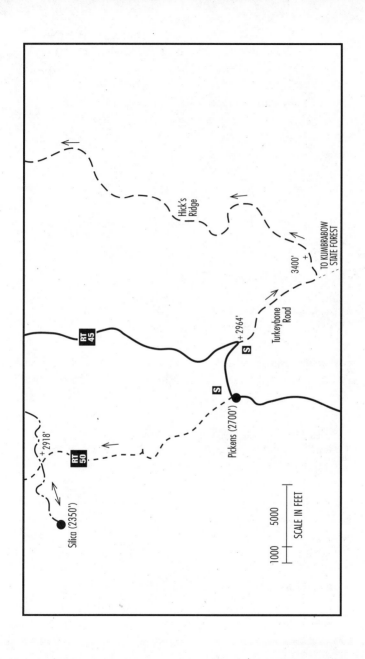

There is an abandoned rail grade that runs from Pickens through Silica and on to Selbyville that would make a wonderful rail trail. The tracks have been taken up on this section. It now has a hard-packed gravel surface that apparently is being used as a road by locals. However, some sections of the old grade have gates, and some of the bridges have been removed. High water is starting to erode the road surface.

TURKEY BONE RD. TO HICK'S RIDGE:

Location: Randolph County.
Length: About 10 miles.
Degree of Difficulty: ****
Scenery: ****
Topo Quad: Pickens.
Elevations (in feet): At start, 2,964; Hick's Ridge, up to 3,400; Helvetia, 2,239.
Footnotes: This trip takes you alongside small farms and a maple sugar operation, then through a section of forest. It may be best to start with a shuttle to Turkeybone Rd.

Description: Turkeybone Rd. veers off to the left from the sharp curve just before you reach Pickens on paved Rt. 45 from Helvetia. This is also the way to Kumbrabow State Forest. Turkeybone is a gravel road that takes you out across the mountains and into Kumbrabow for a ride of 10 miles or better if you want to cross through the forest. For a shorter ride back to Helvetia, take a left off Turkeybone onto Hick's Ridge, which is on the left 1.3 miles in from Rt. 45. This road is a gradual climb of several miles along the ridge to Mike Richter's Sugar

Farm, where maple sap is collected each winter and cooked into wonderful syrup. The road passes the Sugar Farm and enters the woods. Here it becomes rougher, then goes downhill to meet paved Rt. 46. Take a left on Rt. 46 for a mostly downhill ride of a few miles back to Helvetia.

OF INTEREST IN THE AREA

Helvetians love to celebrate, especially at their unique annual festivals. Each festival is distinct, and offers food, parades, and square dances in the community hall. The most traditionally Swiss of the celebrations is *Fasnacht*. This ritual chases away Old Man Winter and welcomes in Spring. Outsiders are invited to join townspeople in donning costumes for a masked ball, after which an effigy of Old Man Winter is burned on a bonfire. *Fasnacht* takes place every February on the Saturday before Ash Wednesday. The local ramp dinner is held at the end of April each year, and means plenty of food and bowls of ramps. The Helvetia Fair is held on the second weekend in September. The fair features a harvest festival with a parade, produce displays, and a square dance in the evening. Swiss dancing and music usually accompany any Helvetian festival.

WHERE TO STAY:

Camping: Camping is available at Kumbrabow State Forest, (304) 335-2219, which is about 20 minutes from

Helvetia; and at Holly River State Park (304) 493-6353, (or toll-free at 1-800-CALL-WVA) which is about 30 minutes away. Both facilities also have cabins for rent.

Bed & Breakfasts: The Beekeeper Inn (304) 924-6435 is run by Eleanor Mailloux, who also has a house in Czar available for rent to guests. For excellent Swiss food, try the local restaurant, the Hutte.

2. ELKINS AND DAVIS AREA

The northern Monongahela National Forest is home to the strange and hauntingly beautiful Dolly Sods, the spectacular Blackwater Falls, and the expansive Canaan Valley. Randolph and Tucker counties offer not only these sights, but also great trails; some of the state's best cross-country and downhill skiing in winter; and hiking, golf, and fishing in warmer weather.

And then there is mountain biking. Much of the attention generated about this sport in West Virginia originated from the numerous paths that snake through the mountains around Canaan and Blackwater Falls — and for good reason. This region offers some of the best mountain biking in the state, as well as the East Coast. The trails are fairly extensive, many of them intersecting with other trails, allowing you to vary your rides in innumerable ways.

Some of the most intensive riding is also done here, not the least of which is during the *24 Hours of Canaan* bike race in early June. For more information on the race, see the end of this chapter. Publicity from the race, as well as the area's great riding, is drawing more mountain bikers each year. However, even though more bikers are finding their way to the region, don't worry too much about hordes of people clogging trails and detracting from your experience. In the peak of summer I came across other bikers only on trails near the most heavily used areas of the parks. To ensure that trails don't suffer from excessive usage, the Forest Service and local mountain bike aficionados actively monitor and reinforce the trails in this area.

I started biking this part of the state just east of Elkins, then worked my way toward Davis. A number of trails in this region are being assembled in a pamphlet by the forest service, which will make a good supplement to this guide. Check the status of the pamphlet by calling their office in Elkins at (304) 636-1800.

Directions: Take Hwy. 33 East (Exit 99) off I-79, about 100 miles north of Charleston. Travel east through Buckhannon and on through Elkins. The biking trails highlighted below are scattered around Elkins and Davis, in Tucker and Randolph counties.

DOBBIN HOUSE TRAIL AT BLACKWATER FALLS:
Location: Davis, Tucker County.
Directions: Trail lies within Blackwater Falls State Park, which is just outside Davis off WV 32. Follow the park signs to the road to Pendleton Lake on your right.
Length: 3.4 mile-loop.
Degree of Difficulty: ***
Scenery: ***
Topo Quads: Blackwater Falls and Mozark Mountain.
Elevation (in feet): Generally around 3,100.
Footnotes: Difficulty rating is due to rocky and rooty conditions at start. One advantage of this trail is that it is near the fabulous Blackwater Falls. I did not include a map of this trail as it is very well marked.

Description: The trailhead is on the left of the park road leading to Pendleton Lake. It loops into the Monongahela National Forest, then back into the park. The trail takes you over the lake dam and a bridge, then enters the woods. The trail is rough at first, then evens out as it reaches a strip-mined area. Follow the trail marked with blue diamonds on trees to make the complete loop. The ride is mostly on level trail that generally stays in the woods and eventually brings you back to the dam. You return to the trailhead for a total ride of 3.4 miles. Other trails exist in the park, but most are for hikers only. The park has a lodge, campground, picnic area, and, perhaps the most often photographed spot in West Virginia, the spectacular Blackwater Falls.

NOTE: The following trails, Bickle Knob, Olson Tower, and the Canaan Mountain Loop, can all be connected for longer rides. At the end of each ride is a section marked Connector Trail. I describe in each trail how to get to the central location of Hendricks. Once in Hendricks, just pick the trail you want to access, and follow that trail's Connector Trail directions in reverse.

BICKLE KNOB:
Location: Elkins, Randolph County.
Directions: Traveling east on U.S. 33 from Elkins, go 4 miles to the exit on the left for Stuart Recreation Area. Follow the signs to the campground.
Length: About a 17 mile loop, depending upon your inclination for getting lost. The alternate long route is 45 to 55 miles.

Degree of Difficulty: ****
Scenery: ***
Topo Quads: Elkins and Bowden; long route requires
Parsons map.
Elevations (in feet): Stuart Campground, 2,100;
Bickle Knob, 4,000; Baker Sods, 2,800-3,000.
Footnotes: The scenery varies in this region, from
wooded areas, to small pastures, to the open sods. Diffi-
culty rating is based on a long initial climb and the length
of the trail.

This is a wildlife-sensitive area as defined by state and
federal biologists, and should be ridden with caution or
avoided entirely during spring and early summer. Too
much intrusion in the wildlife management area may
affect breeding and nesting animals. Use proper judge-
ment. Also, drainage is poor on some of the trail sections.
It is best to avoid those sections in rainy weather. For
more information on the status of Baker Sods, call the
National Forest Service Office in Elkins at (304) 636-
1800.

Description: I started this trail from the campground at
the Stuart Recreation Area. From the campground, pedal
back to the entrance and take FR 91, a marked gravel
road, up to Bickle Knob, a climb of 4.2 miles. On the
way up to Bickle Knob you'll see several smaller trails that
shoot off FR 91, but stay straight. At about 4.1 miles is a
fork at FR 793. Stay on FR 91 by going left. Just after
this left is another fork. Another left here takes you a
short distance to the end of the road at the top of the
knob, which offers a great view. A right takes you further
into the loop. About .5 mile after Bickle Knob, take a left

onto FR 774. This goes downhill for 2 miles to another fork. At the fork go left again onto FR 132, which takes you through Baker Sods.

This is a wildlife management area of about 70 acres. FR 132 is dirt and gravel, with relatively easy riding. The road enters the grassy management area. Tire tracks weave through the grass in the Sods, but you should be able to distinguish the main set of tracks making their way through the center. Stay on the center set of tracks, which take you through the grassland. Woods begin on the opposite side of the sods, where you catch FR 798. FR 798 alternates between double and single track, and can be muddy. It's mostly downhill for over 1 mile until you reach gravel again. FR 798 goes downhill for 2 more miles to an intersection with Rt. 6 at Shavers Fork River. Take a left here, then a left at the fork just down the road. Follow Rt. 6, which parallels Shavers Fork River. It is 6 miles back to the Stuart Campground. This last leg is mostly level with just a few climbs.

LONG ROUTE: Those into long distance riding should take the much longer alternative route around Baker Sods. You work your way north on forest roads to the Fernow Experimental Forest, then cut west over to Rt. 6, and then down along Shavers Fork River. This is around 45 to 55 miles, or three times as long a trip as the route through the Baker Sods, so plan accordingly. You'll also need the Parsons topo map.

Directions: For this route, at the fork on FR 774, instead of turning left toward the Baker Sods on FR 132, go right on FR 132 East. You'll take three right forks within the

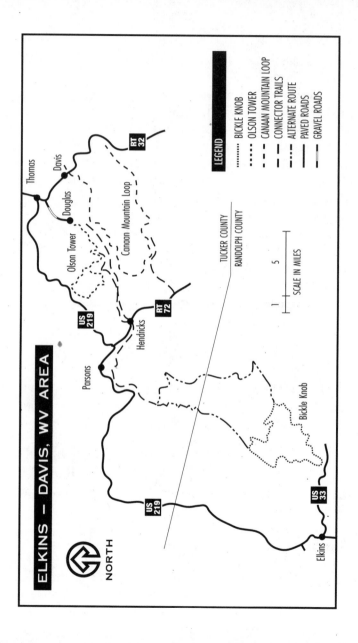

ELKINS – DAVIS, WV AREA

NORTH

Thomas
Davis
Douglas
Olson Tower
Canaan Mountain Loop
RT 32
Parsons
Hendricks
RT 72
US 219
US 219
Bickle Knob
US 33
Elkins

TUCKER COUNTY
RANDOLPH COUNTY

SCALE IN MILES
1   5

LEGEND

····· BICKLE KNOB
····· OLSON TOWER
—··— CANAAN MOUNTAIN LOOP
— — CONNECTOR TRAILS
—·— ALTERNATE ROUTE
—— PAVED ROADS
—— GRAVEL ROADS

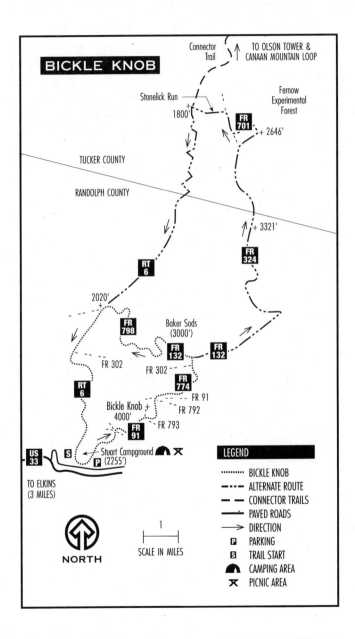

first .75 mile, then one left fork. At around 2 miles down
FR 132, the road takes a sharp left and becomes FR 324.
Nine or 10 miles down FR 324 go left at the fork.
Within the next mile, take two more left forks. This puts
you on Stonelick Run, which requires walking due to
overgrowth and the steep trail. Stonelick Run will drop
you to Rt. 6, (Shavers Fork) where you go left and
eventually return to Stuart Campground.

CONNECTOR TRAIL: To connect with Olson Tower
or Canaan Mountain Loop via Hendricks, take a right at
Shavers Fork on Rt. 6. As you approach Parsons, go right
at the fork and pick up the Black Fork Trail. You will
cross a swinging bridge, on your left, to enter Hendricks.

Olson Tower Lookout/Canyon Rim Trail:
Location: Douglas, Tucker County.
Directions: Traveling on WV 32 from Davis, take Rt. 27
on the left just before Thomas, then drive a couple of
miles until you cross the second bridge. Park here, and
FR 18 — a marked, gravel road — heads uphill in front
of you.
Length: About 18 miles out-and-back.
Degree of Difficulty: ***
Scenery: ****
Topo quad: Mozark Mountain and Lead Mine.
Elevations (in feet): Douglas, 2,800; Olson Tower,
3,653; Canyon Rim Trail, 3,600 down to 3,100.
Footnotes: Difficulty rating is due to modest climbs and
length of trail. Scenery includes wooded hillsides,
expansive views of Blackwater Canyon, and the view from

Olson Tower. This is a moderately easy ride that combines rarely traveled forest roads with a scenic trail overlooking Blackwater Canyon. The total trip is about 18 miles if started at Douglas. A friend and I started this trail on a cool morning, before the fog had lifted from the mountain. At several points I spotted deer bounding through the mist. We also heard a turkey gobbling as we came back down the hill. Neither of these experiences is uncommon in West Virginia woodlands.

Description: FR 18 is a gradual climb along a wooded mountainside. To the left are occasional views of the gorge below. On the way up there is an overlook on the left at 5.2 miles from the parking spot. There should be a brown Forest Service sign on your right, and a yellow paint mark on the boulder to your left. From here you have a great view of Blackwater Canyon, and can hear the river crashing through the underbrush below. At the 7.3 mile mark, take a left onto FR 717. FR 717 is a slightly steeper climb of over 1.5 miles, taking you to Olson Tower. You reach the mountain top after biking 9 miles from the parking spot in Douglas. The tower, with an elevation of 3653 feet, offers views of the countryside for miles around. You'll find a water pump and a picnic area here.

An alternative to retracing your path back to FR 18 is to catch Canyon Rim Trail, which is .2 miles down the hill on your right as you begin to descend from Olson Tower. This single track is fun and mostly downhill. Area bike enthusiasts have maintained this trail to protect it from overuse. There are rocky spots and some boggy areas that can be sloppy in wet weather, which is common

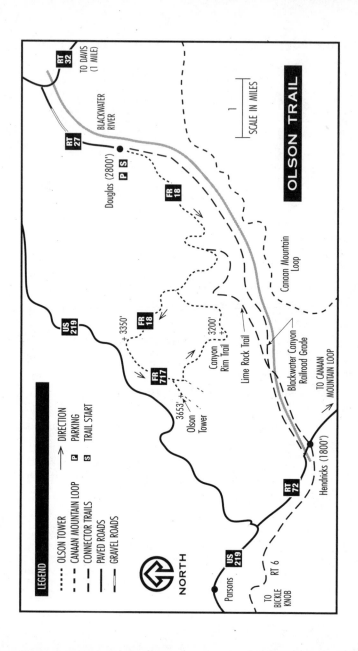

OLSON TRAIL

LEGEND

⋯⋯ OLSON TOWER
····· CANAAN MOUNTAIN LOOP
--- CONNECTOR TRAILS
—— PAVED ROADS
═══ GRAVEL ROADS

→ DIRECTION
P PARKING
S TRAIL START

NORTH

SCALE IN MILES

RT 32
TO DAVIS (1 MILE)

BLACKWATER RIVER

RT 27

Douglas (2800')
P S

FR 18

FR 18
+ 3350'

US 219

FR 717
3653' +
Olson Tower

Canyon Rim Trail
3200' +

Lime Rock Trail

Blackwater Canyon Railroad Grade

Canaan Mountain Loop

TO CANAAN MOUNTAIN LOOP

RT 72
Hendricks (1800')

US 219
Parsons

RT 6

TO BICKLE KNOB

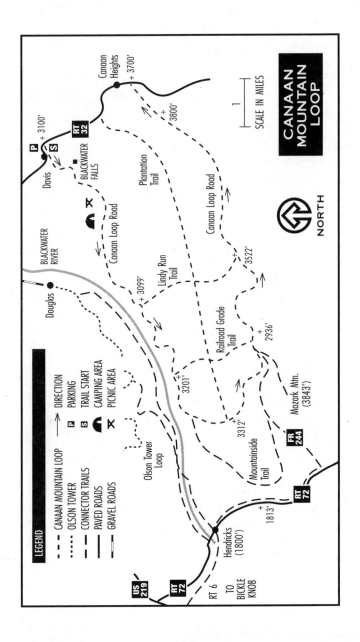

CANAAN MOUNTAIN LOOP

NORTH

SCALE IN MILES

LEGEND
- CANAAN MOUNTAIN LOOP
- OLSON TOWER
- CONNECTOR TRAILS
- PAVED ROADS
- GRAVEL ROADS

→ DIRECTION
P PARKING
S TRAIL START
☾ CAMPING AREA
⚲ PICNIC AREA

Canaan Heights + 3700'
+ 3800'

Davis + 3100'
RT 32
P
S
BLACKWATER FALLS

BLACKWATER RIVER

Douglas

Canaan Loop Road
Plantation Trail
Canaan Loop Road
+ 3099'
Lindy Run Trail
+ 3522'
Railroad Grade Trail
+ 2936'
Mozark Mtn. (3843')
FR 244

+ 3201'
+ 3312'
Mountainside Trail

Olson Tower Loop

Hendricks (1800')
+ 1813'
RT 72
US 219
RT 72
RT 6 TO BICKLE KNOB

here. At 11 miles from the start — or 1.8 miles from the turnoff at Olson Tower — is a waterfall in a rhododendron thicket on the right. At 12.3 miles, you come to two creeks; the second, larger one is just a few yards past the first. Just after you cross the second creek you'll hit FR 18. Take a right here for a downhill ride to the parking spot, ending the trip at 17.8 miles.

If it has rained recently, the last creek crossing on Canyon Rim Trail might be rough and could force you to backtrack to Olson Tower. You can avoid this by checking the creek level on your way up the hill. At 5.5 miles on the left is the lower intersection of Canyon Rim Trail. Stop here and walk down the trail about 50 yards until you can check for a safe crossing.

CONNECTOR TRAILS: Approximately 2.5 miles from the start in Douglas, is Lime Rock Trail, on the left. This trail starts south, turns north, then south again, and winds up in Hendricks. There is only one turn, (left) about 1 mile into Lime Rock Trail. At Hendricks, you have a few options. You can come back on the Blackwater Canyon Railroad Grade, which is a steady, mellow uphill back to your car in Douglas. You can also ride to Bickle Knob or take the Canaan Mountain Loop.

CANAAN MOUNTAIN LOOP:
Location: Tucker County.
Directions: This ride starts in downtown Davis.
Length: From 9 to 30 miles, depending on your route(s).
Degree of Difficulty: *** or ****
Scenery: *****

Topo Quads: Davis, Blackwater Falls, and Mozark Mountain.

Elevations (in feet): From a low of 2,935 at Red Run, to a high of 3,843 at Mozark Mountain.

Footnotes: This loop has numerous options and offshoots for exploring, all of which encircle Canaan Loop Rd. Canaan Loop Rd. is a dirt road which makes for good riding by itself. However, for some great single track, I recommend getting off and exploring the inner trails. This area is a wonderful hardwood forest. A spruce plantation was planted here in the 1930's to cover up the earlier clearcuts of the region. Now a majestic forest — of spruce, birch, beech, and sugar maple — towers over the numerous rhododendron thickets.

Description: In Davis, I recommend first pigging out on great pizza at Sirianni's, and then checking out Blackwater Bikes. Both are on Main Street. To start the ride, head south down Main Street (Rt. 32) toward the convenience store. Just past the store, the road bears right and crosses the Blue Bridge. Immediately after the bridge, take the dirt road to your right; this follows the Blackwater River. Take this old railroad grade just past a small pond; at the fork go right on a rocky double track. Continue through a stream, and to an intersection at 2 miles. Take a left onto the paved road into Blackwater Falls State Park. Stay on the paved road for about 2 miles (bikes are prohibited in most of the park). At 4.5 miles the paved road forks. Left is toward the cabins, but instead go right onto the road marked Sled Run. This road soon turns to dirt and becomes Canaan Loop Rd. You can stay on this road the whole way and do some great miles. You can also try some of the fabulous single track options.

At 6 miles, past Lindy Run water crossing and up a short hill, is a trail marker on the left for *Lindy Run Trail*. This is a tough single track that goes uphill and roughly cuts the Canaan Loop in half. You can skip Lindy Run at this point, and later pick it up from the backside of the loop. It's easier and downhill to start Lindy Run from the back. (See mile 16.) Continuing on Canaan Loop Rd., go past Lindy Run to *Railroad Grade Trail* at 7.5 miles on your left. This is a rugged but gorgeous trail that gets tougher as you go.

At 9.5 miles on the right is *Mountainside Trail*. This is a rough, overgrown rail grade that leads down a mountain and intersects FR 244. A right onto FR 244 will take you down to the Dry Fork River, and Rt. 72. You can use this to access and connect with Bickle Knob or Olson Tower.

At 10.5 miles on the left is *Plantation Trail*, which bisects the loop long ways. This trail can be hard to find, as the wooden sign on the left is set back from the road. This is a technical, rough, 9 mile trail over bogs, boulders, and roots. It takes you back to Canaan Mountain Loop near Rt. 32. You can do the whole trail, or cut onto any of the many trails that intersect it.

Just up the road from Plantation Trail is a well-marked sign for *Table Rock Overlook*, which plunges down to the right and the Dry Fork River. This trail isn't recommended unless you enjoy walking your bike while squeezing the brakes.

At 11 miles is a downhill to Red Run. Take this 2 mile downhill slowly, and enjoy the great scenery. At 12.5 miles, on a sharply angled right, is *FR 244*. This is the road I recommend (over Table Rock or Mountainside Trail) to connect with the other trails in the area. Taking FR 244, you drop 1300 feet to Dry Fork River and Rt. 72. Go right on paved Rt. 72 for approximately 4 miles into Hendricks.

Back on Canaan Loop Rd., at 13 miles at the bottom of the hill, is an intersection. Keep straight and start the 7 mile, 825 foot climb back. At 13.5 miles on the left is *Railroad Grade Trail* (see 7.5 miles). It's a steep climb before falling and intersecting Plantation Trail.

At 16 miles on the left with a wooden sign is *Lindy Run Trail* (see mile 6). It's easier from this end but still technical single track.

At 20 miles Canaan Loop Rd. finally hits Rt. 32. Go left and head back toward the Blue Bridge and downtown Davis.

CONNECTOR TRAIL: See FR 244 above at 11 miles.

MORE RIDING IN THE AREA:

There are plenty of other trails in the Canaan area that provide mountain bikers with a variety of challenges. Blackwater Bikes in Davis offers a number of tours, as well as rentals, a local trail guide, and bike servicing. In the Elkins area, Elkins Bikeworks offers the same services for trails in Randolph County. Owner Karen Carper also has a hostel with low-cost rooms.

A number of races are held each year in the Canaan area, drawing people from across the country. One of the premier mountain biking races in the country — *The 24*

Hours of Canaan Team Relay Race — takes place in early June near Davis. This race is a unique format for mountain bike racing. The creator and director of the event, Laird Knight, says the premise of the race was loosely based on the famous *24 Hours of LeMans* auto race. The race encourages team riding among otherwise loosely organized groups of friends, casual riders, and racers, and is mainly for fun. Fun? Being awoken at 3 a.m. by your teammate to race down the mountains of West Virginia in the dark? Sure!

The race runs from noon on Saturday until noon on Sunday. Racers compete on either 4 or 5 person teams. There are about seven different classes for riders to enter. The race started in 1992 with 32 teams finishing the course. Currently the limit is 300 teams. Everything I hear about this race makes it sound like something every (crazy) mountain biker has to try. From the *LeMans*-style start where the racers sprint to their bikes to the idea of racing on these piles of rocks at night; from the super-highly developed (and highly individual) strategies of each team to the 24-hour non-stop wackiness — who can resist? Laird unabashedly says that if you enter the race, you won't be disappointed. At the very least, try it the first time as a spectator or volunteer. If you miss it this year, you'll probably read about it later and be sorry you missed it.

To make sure you get in on the most exciting mountain bike race in West Virginia, contact Laird Knight at Granny Gear Productions, P.O. Box 189, Davis, WV 26260, (304) 259-5533.

WHERE TO STAY:

Camping: There is a 25 unit campground at Stuart Recreation Area off U.S. 33, 4 miles east of Elkins. Bear Heaven has an 8 unit campground, which is also off U.S. 33 east of Elkins. Canaan and Blackwater Falls State Parks also have campgrounds. Call 1-800-CALL-WVA for specific information and reservations.

Bed & Breakfasts and Inns: Meyer House (304) 259-5451, White Oak B&B (304) 478-4705, and Bright Morning Inn (304) 259-5119 in Davis; Tunnel Mountain B&B (304) 636-1684, The Retreat at Buffalo Run (304) 636-2960, Mountain Splendor Inn (304) 636-8111, Wayside Inn (304) 636-1618, and The Cheat Mountain Lodge (304) 636-2301, in and around Elkins.

Lodges: Canaan and Blackwater Falls State Parks both have lodges. Call the state's toll-free tourism number (1-800-CALL-WVA) for rates and reservations.

3. CRANBERRY BACK COUNTRY

First I heard the rustle, then I saw a black, dog-sized figure trot away from the trail. Close behind was a second figure, then a third. Just as the cubs reached their mother, I realized I'd had the good fortune of spotting a black bear family out for a Sunday stroll. Such sightings are not unusual in the Cranberry back country, a unique and beautiful wilderness area. From the bizarre Cranberry Glades to the tumbling Tea Creek and the spectacular Highlands Scenic Highway, the back country makes for great mountain biking and hiking. Because of the relatively high altitude, weather is more moderate in summer and carries a harsher bite in winter than in many parts of West Virginia. This is a wonderful part of the state to see wildflowers and take in broad views of the surrounding mountains and valleys.

Well-marked trails contribute to the great biking here. It's probably best to begin any back country adventure by first stopping at the Cranberry Visitor's Center, which is about 21 miles east of Richwood on WV 39/55. At the Visitor's Center you can get maps and brochures. In the brochures you can read about the glades, which are acidic wetlands more commonly found in the northern U.S. and Canada. The glades are made up of four bogs that are filled with unusual plant life. A good way to see some of the glades is by taking the .5 mile hike along the Cranberry Glades boardwalk, which is near the Visitor's Center.

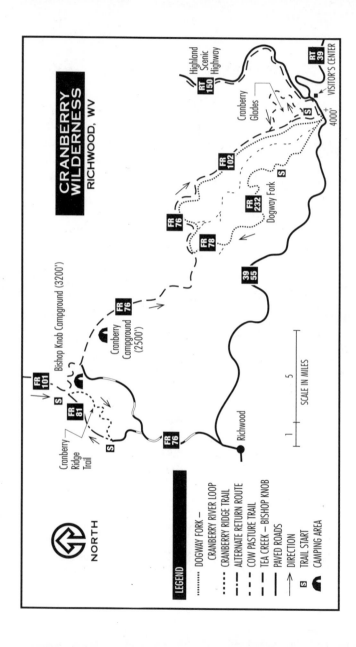

CRANBERRY WILDERNESS
RICHWOOD, WV

NORTH

LEGEND

DOGWAY FORK –
CRANBERRY RIVER LOOP
CRANBERRY RIDGE TRAIL
ALTERNATE RETURN ROUTE
COW PASTURE TRAIL
TEA CREEK – BISHOP KNOB
PAVED ROADS
DIRECTION
TRAIL START
CAMPING AREA

Bishop Knob Campground (3200')

FR 101

FR 81

Cranberry Ridge Trail

S

S

FR 76

Cranberry Campground (2500')

FR 76

39 55

Richwood

SCALE IN MILES
1   5

FR 76

FR 78

FR 232

Dogway Fork

FR 102

S

Cranberry Glades

RT 150

Highland Scenic Highway

RT 39

S

4000'

VISITOR'S CENTER

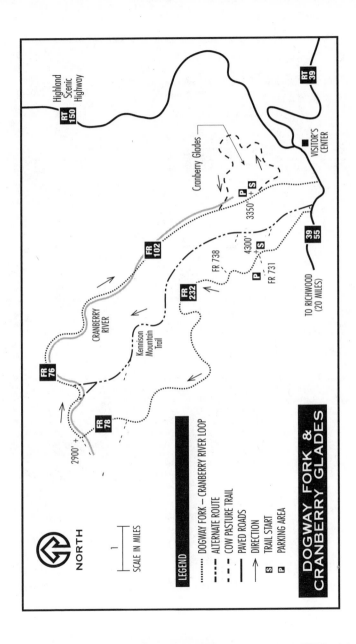

NORTH

1
SCALE IN MILES

LEGEND

········· DOGWAY FORK – CRANBERRY RIVER LOOP
─·─·─ ALTERNATE ROUTE
─ ─ ─ COW PASTURE TRAIL
─── PAVED ROADS
→ DIRECTION
Ⓢ TRAIL START
Ⓟ PARKING AREA

**DOGWAY FORK &
CRANBERRY GLADES**

Highland
Scenic
Highway

RT
150

RT
39

VISITOR'S
CENTER

Cranberry Glades

Ⓟ Ⓢ
3350' +

FR
102

FR
738

4300'
Ⓟ + Ⓢ
FR 731

39
55

TO RICHWOOD
(20 MILES)

FR
232

CRANBERRY
RIVER

Kennison
Mountain
Trail

FR
76

FR
78

2900' +

While the Cranberry Glades Botanical Area and the Cranberry Wilderness themselves are off limits to bicyclists, there still is plenty of ground to cover in the area. Some short and long loops are possible, but it's better to have a shuttle system to get to most of the trails without having to retrace your tracks.

I have ridden both easy and difficult trails in the Cranberry, some with mountain climbs and some with gentle river grades. Whatever your skill level, there is a path to accommodate you. Listed below are trail summaries for the region.

DOGWAY FORK/CRANBERRY RIVER LOOP:

Location: Pocahontas County, near Cranberry Visitor's Center.

Directions: Take WV 39/55 East from Richwood for about 20 miles. Go left on FR 232, or Dogway Fork Road. Take it for about 1 mile to a gate. There is a gravel area on the left for parking.

Length: 24.2 mile loop.

Degree of Difficulty: ***

Scenery: *****

Topo Quads: Webster Springs SW and SE, and Lobelia.

Elevations (in feet): Dogway Fork start, 4,300; at Cranberry River, 2,900; Glades area, 3,300-3,400.

Footnotes: Difficulty rating is due to length. Climbs are gradual, with the exception of a short stretch up Kennison Mountain. Scenery is wooded down to the river, then great river views appear until you head up toward the glades.

Description: All of this loop, except for a short stretch along paved WV 39/55, is on forest roads. You start by taking FR 232 beyond the gate. The trip down to the Cranberry River is a glorious 9 mile downhill. Twice along this route I accidentally spooked deer with fawns. At about 1.75 miles take a left at the fork. At 7.3 miles is a bridge that makes a nice place to stop, stretch, and enjoy the scenery. Rocks have veins of water tumbling past them, and ferns carpet the forest floor. In July the rhododendron blooms break the greenery with sprays of pink.

FR 232 eventually changes its name to FR 78. At 8.9 miles, you reach the Cranberry River and the intersection with the river road, or FR 76. Take a right on FR 76, which turns into FR 102 after a couple of miles. FR 102 takes you along the South Fork of the Cranberry. You'll encounter a few intersections, but keep straight on the main trail and follow the river on FR 102. You reach a road gate at 18.7 miles. Continue past the gate and past Cranberry Glades Boardwalk until you hit WV 39/55. Take a right on 39/55, where you huff it up to the top of Kennison Mountain. You continue down the other side a short distance until you reach Dogway Fork Rd. on your right. You'll reach your parking spot after a climb of just over 1 mile, for a total trip of 24.2 miles. An alternative to having the climbs at the end of the trip would be to park at the Glades boardwalk, then proceed on WV 39/55 to Dogway and up to the gate.

ALTERNATE ROUTE - KENNISON MOUNTAIN TRAIL: An alternative to taking FR 232 is to go off road onto the Kennison Mountain Trail. This trail goes for about 10 miles from the top of Kennison Mountain on WV 39/55 until it reaches the Cranberry River. The trail is accessed on WV 39/55, just east of FR 232 on the left. Just after you start, take the fork on your right. Take another right at about 7 miles. Go straight, passing a sharp switchback on the right. Go right again at the final fork down to the river. Watch for some steep descents as the trail approaches the river. Unless you want to return the same route, you must cross the Cranberry. This isn't a major challenge if there is an average flow, but could be a problem with high water. The Cranberry River Rd. is just over the river. You can go right or left to return to the start; they're about the same distance. You can go right and head toward FR 102 and come back past the glades. If you go left on Cranberry River Rd., a short ways down you'll go left again on FR 78, and return through Dogway.

COW PASTURE TRAIL:

Location: Pocahontas County, near Cranberry Glades Boardwalk.

Directions: On Hwy 39/55 East, 25 miles east of Richwood, just before the Cranberry Glades Visitors' Center, the Cranberry Glades Boardwalk appears on your left. From the boardwalk lot, go left and uphill .2 mile on the paved road until you see the Cow Pasture sign on your left.

Length: 7.5 mile loop.

Degree of Difficulty: **

Scenery: ****

Topo Quad: Lobelia.

Elevation (in feet): Mostly in 3,400 range.

Footnotes: This ride is an easy and fun way to experience

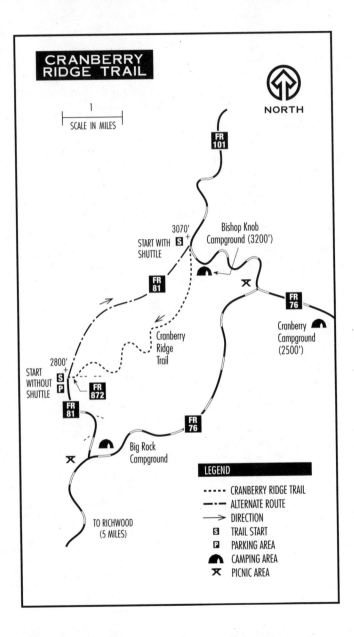

CRANBERRY RIDGE TRAIL

NORTH

1
SCALE IN MILES

FR 101

3070'
START WITH SHUTTLE · S +

Bishop Knob Campground (3200')

FR 81

FR 76

Cranberry Campground (2500')

Cranberry Ridge Trail

2800'
START WITHOUT SHUTTLE · S P +

FR 872

FR 81

FR 76

Big Rock Campground

TO RICHWOOD (5 MILES)

LEGEND

····· CRANBERRY RIDGE TRAIL
—·—· ALTERNATE ROUTE
—→ DIRECTION
S TRAIL START
P PARKING AREA
⌂ CAMPING AREA
✕ PICNIC AREA

the glades. The scenery is varied; you'll travel through woods, pastures, and swampy bogs. Small, wooden bridges take you over several creeks, where you can see beaver and muskrat. Deer and bear tracks dotted the trail in late July. The glades area is noted for bird watching, and the unique plant life merits close examination.

Description: Cow Pasture is a relatively short trail that can be made into a loop by parking at the Cranberry Glades Boardwalk lot. The trail takes you along a narrow seam between the botanical area and the wilderness area, both of which are off limits to bikers. The trail is narrow but level here, passing through woods until it opens up to a grassy, marshy area. At the 1 mile mark from where you started at the lot, there are signs and a photo of a prison camp that stood there until 1959. At the prison camp signs, take a left and follow the well marked blue diamond symbols. The trail can be wet and muddy in spots. Where it is wet, walk your bike to keep from damaging the trail. At about 6.3 miles from where you started near the boardwalk, you emerge from the woods onto FR 102. Take a left here and continue back up to the boardwalk, for a total trip of 7.5 miles.

CRANBERRY RIDGE TRAIL:
Location: Off FR 81 near Bishop Knob.
Directions: Go east on WV 39/55 just outside Richwood until you see WV 76, or Cranberry River Rd., on your left. Take WV 76 until it turns into FR 76, then travel a few more miles until you reach FR 81 on your left. A couple of miles up FR 81 will be FR 872 on your right,

which has a gate at the entrance. Either park here and have someone shuttle you up to the Cranberry Ridge Trail, which is marked on your right, or bike uphill the couple of miles to the trail.

Length: 4-7 mile loop, depending on how much you want to bike.

Degree of Difficulty: ***

Scenery: ***

Topo Quads: Camden-on-Gauley and Webster Springs SW.

Elevations (in feet): From 3,070 to about 2,800 at lower FR 81.

Footnotes: This trail starts just below the top of Bishop Knob and takes you past the Glade Pond. It was along this trail that I encountered a bear family. The mother and three cubs acknowledged my intrusion, then trotted off into the woods.

Description: Either shuttle or climb FR 81 up to FR 872 on the right. The trail begins as single track, then widens as it becomes an old logging road around the 1.5 mile mark. Follow the blue diamond markers as you reach intersections, and you'll have no trouble following the trail. There are some roots and rocks along the trail, but it is generally easy, with only one noteworthy uphill of just over .2 mile. At about the 3 mile mark Glade Pond is off to the right. A short distance past the pond, the trail shoots uphill to the left, then back downhill until it reaches FR 81. From here, you can continue on the trail for another 2 miles to a dead end, or take a right and go downhill a short distance until you reach the parking spot at FR 872.

Another option is to start out at Bishop Knob Campground. In the campground you need to work your way into the southwest corner to pick up Cranberry Ridge Trail. The easiest way to do this is to stay left at all options on the road. In the back of the campground just as you start to head back the other way, is Cranberry Ridge Trail on your right.

OF INTEREST IN THE AREA:

There are a number of "hiking only" trails through the glades that can bring you into close contact with a truly unique environment. The Visitor's Center has good information material about the glades. Some of the area rivers — the Cherry, Cranberry and Williams — are excellent trout streams. A number of shelters and campsites dot the Cranberry banks between the glades boardwalk and the Cranberry Campground at the lower gate, some 18 miles downstream. For information on other attractions in the area, call the Pocahontas County Commission at 1-800-336-7009.

WHERE TO STAY:

Camping: Well-maintained campsites at Big Rock, Summit Lake, Bishop Knob, Cranberry, Tea Creek, and Day Run campgrounds all offer good access to the Cranberry back country. They all are reached by taking forest roads off WV 39/55 or Highlands Scenic Highway from the Visitor's Center.

Bed & Breakfasts: The Elk River Inn (304) 572-3771 in Slatyfork has an excellent restaurant. This B&B is run by Gil Willis, who also runs the Elk River Touring Center. The latter offers guided bike tours in the area and bike servicing. For more B&B's try: located in Cass, Shay Inn B&B (304) 572-3771; in or near Marlinton, Jerico B&B (304) 799-6241, The Old Clark Inn (304) 799-6377, The Guesthouse (304) 799-6711, and the Carriage House Inn (304) 799-6706; outside of Hillsboro, The Current B&B (304) 653-4722 and Yew Mountain Lodge (304) 653-4821.

4. TEA CREEK

The Tea Creek trails offer riding challenges ranging from highly technical rides to an easy roll along the Williams River. The car trip to Tea Creek from the Cranberry Visitor's Center is one to remember, with a number of overlooks offering views of the Cranberry Glades and surrounding mountains and valleys. The highway itself has little traffic, making it good for road biking. Its hills would also challenge a mountain biker.

A good map of the Tea Creek area is available at the Cranberry Visitor's Center. I biked partially along the Tea Creek Trail, the Williams River Trail, and the Bannock Shoals Run Trail by starting at the Tea Creek campground. I also biked in on the Gauley Mountain Trail from FR 24, then took Bear Pen Ridge and the upper Tea Creek Trails.

Directions: Take WV 39/55 East from Richwood to the Cranberry Visitor's Center. Take a left on Highland Scenic Highway, go about 15 miles to FR 86. Go left on FR 86. The Tea Creek Campground appears shortly on the right.

TRAILS FROM TEA CREEK CAMPGROUND:
Location: Pocahontas County, off Highland Scenic Highway.

Length: Varies depending on trail and choice of loops.
Degree of Difficulty: Ranges from * on the Williams River Trail to **** on several of the trails that weave into the mountains.
Scenery: ***
Topo Quads: Sharp Knob and Woodrow.
Elevations (in feet): Campground, 3,000; mountain trails up to 4,300.
Footnotes: Difficulty rating is based on length, climbs, and obstacles on trails.

Description: The Williams River Trail is at the right of the campground entrance, and is a relatively easy, scenic, 2.2 mile out-and-back that takes you along the river to the Handley Public Hunting and Fishing Area. Biologists recommend that bikers not enter the hunting and fishing area, so as not to disturb mating and nesting animals.

Bannock Shoals (FR 135) is somewhat longer (3.8 miles) and is a gravel forest road with some climbs through wooded hills.

The Tea Creek Trail is more challenging, as it is sprinkled with rocks, roots and old railroad ties. It is an uncomfortable ride unless you enjoy such obstacles. Numerous trails branch off Tea Creek Trail and provide additional exploring. Each of these trails connects with others in the area, allowing small and large loops to be linked for longer rides.

TRAILS FROM FR 24 (GAULEY MOUNTAIN ROAD):
Location: Pocahontas County.
Length: 7.5 miles if you do the Gauley Mountain/Bear

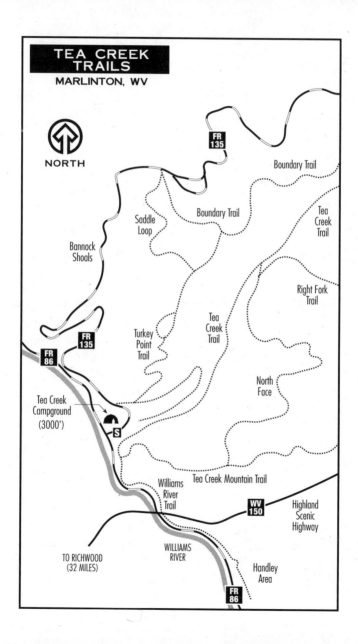

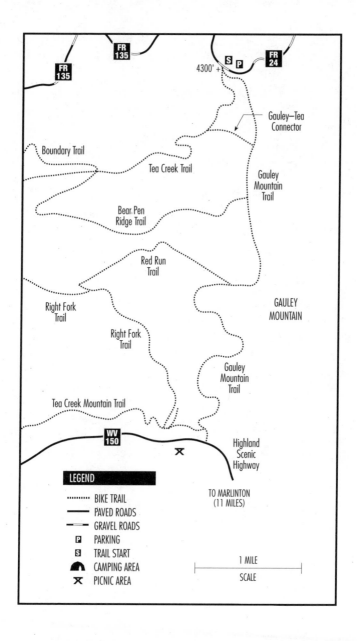

FR 135

FR 135

S P

FR 24

4300' +

Gauley–Tea
Connector

Boundary Trail

Tea Creek Trail

Gauley
Mountain
Trail

Bear Pen
Ridge Trail

Red Run
Trail

Right Fork
Trail

GAULEY
MOUNTAIN

Right Fork
Trail

Gauley
Mountain
Trail

Tea Creek Mountain Trail

WV 150

Highland
Scenic
Highway

TO MARLINTON
(11 MILES)

LEGEND

.... BIKE TRAIL

———— PAVED ROADS

———— GRAVEL ROADS

P   PARKING

S   TRAIL START

🏕   CAMPING AREA

✕   PICNIC AREA

1 MILE

SCALE

Pen Ridge/Tea Creek Trail loop, or longer if you want to add other Tea Creek trails that connect to the Gauley Mountain Trail.

Degree of Difficulty: Generally *** and ****
Scenery: ***
Topo Quad: Sharp Knob.
Elevations (in feet): Trailhead on FR 24, just under 4,300; Tea Creek Trail, 3,100-3,200.

Description: An alternative to entering the Tea Creek area from the campground is to take FR 24 to the Gauley Mountain and Tea Creek trailheads. If you are traveling north on U.S. 219, FR 24 is on the left about 1.5 miles before you reach the Elk River Touring Center in Slatyfork. The road is gravel, and has a concrete bridge at the start. Take this road uphill for 3.5 miles to reach the Gauley Mountain Trail on your left. There is parking here for a couple of vehicles.

The Gauley Mountain Trail is a mostly level trail that goes for about 5 miles across the mountain to the Highland Scenic Highway. It can be ridden as an out-and-back, or used to access other Tea Creek trails. I rode this trail for about 1.5 miles, then took the Bear Pen Ridge Trail on the right. This is a rocky trail at the start. It seems like a creek bed in some spots as water drains here from Gauley Mountain. About .5 mile in, the trail begins to open up, but there are soupy areas that swallow up bike tires. Better to walk around these than cause potential trail damage. Surface conditions improve at about 2.7 miles.

At 3.2 miles into the ride, there is a shelter — an open-faced, wooden building suitable for camping.

Another rocky patch on Bear Pen Ridge Trail appears at 3.7 miles, and .1 mile beyond that you begin an arm-numbing downhill ride for 1 mile. At 4.8 miles Bear Pen Ridge intersects with Tea Creek and the Tea Creek Trail. There are several options here. You can take a left and ride the Tea Creek Trail 4.3 miles down to the campground, or go straight to the Boundary Trail and also work your way down to the campground. These options require either a shuttle from the campground, or a trip back uphill to the Gauley Mountain Trail.

The Elk River Touring Center recommended a loop that requires staying on Bear Pen Ridge after crossing Tea Creek. This is what I did. About 5 miles into the trail is a washout. Just beyond it FR 135 appears on the right. Travel about 6 miles on FR 135 until you reach FR 24, where you take a right and travel a couple of miles back to your car at the Gauley Mountain trailhead. I started on this loop, but a stick jammed into my derailleur and snapped it off. I backtracked to the Tea Creek Trail and took it out to FR 24. This option gives you a loop off of Bear Pen Ridge for about 7.5 miles total.

The upper part of the Tea Creek Trail from Bear Pen is rough at the start, with rocks and old rail ties for the first .5 mile. The trail then clears and dries up somewhat. At 1.2 miles from Bear Pen Ridge there is a sharp switchback to the right — keep your eyes on the marked trees. At 1.7 miles is an intersection with the Tea Creek Connector Trail, which hits the Gauley Mountain Trail just over .5 away. If you choose to go left at this intersection and continue on the Tea Creek Trail, you have about a .2 mile climb on a rocky path. Two miles up Tea Creek Trail from where it crossed Bear Pen Ridge, you'll find a shelter, picnic table, and campfire spot. At 2.7 miles you are back at FR 24. Take a right here and go a couple 100 yards to get to your car at the Gauley Mountain trailhead.

More information on Tea Creek is available at Elk River Touring Center (304-572-3771), which is in Slatyfork at the end of the Scenic Highway.

FR 86 FROM TEA CREEK TO BISHOP KNOB/ CRANBERRY CAMPGROUNDS:

Location: Pocahontas County.
Length: About 26 miles with shuttle, or over 50 miles without.
Degree of Difficulty: ***
Scenery: ****
Topo Quads: Webster Springs, Webster Springs SW, Webster Springs SE, and Woodrow.
Elevations (in feet): Tea Creek Campground, 3,000; Dyer, 2,200-2,300; Bishop Knob, 3,200; Cranberry Campground, 2,500.
Footnotes: Difficulty rating is based on length and climb at Bishop Knob. Scenery is beautiful along the Williams and Cranberry Rivers.

Description: Another route from Tea Creek, this ride involves a shuttle if you want to keep it under 30 miles. Otherwise it's a challenging 50-plus mile ride. By taking a right on FR 86 as you exit Tea Creek Campground, you travel alongside some beautiful stretches of the Williams River, through the community of Dyer, over Bishop Knob, and down to the Cranberry Campground. From Tea Creek, the gravel forest road FR 86 follows the grade

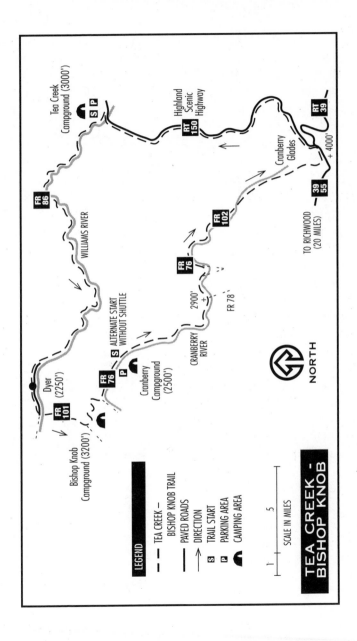

TEA CREEK - BISHOP KNOB

LEGEND

– – – TEA CREEK – BISHOP KNOB TRAIL
——— PAVED ROADS
——→ DIRECTION
S TRAIL START
P PARKING AREA
◖ CAMPING AREA

1   5
SCALE IN MILES

NORTH

Tea Creek Campground (3000')
S P

Highland Scenic Highway
RT 150

RT 39
+ 4000'

Cranberry Glades

FR 86

FR 102

WILLIAMS RIVER

FR 76

39 55

TO RICHWOOD (20 MILES)

2900'
FR 78

CRANBERRY RIVER

ALTERNATE START WITHOUT SHUTTLE
S
P

Cranberry Campground (2500')

FR 76

Dyer (2250')
FR 101

Bishop Knob Campground (3200')

of the river for about 10 miles. It crosses a bridge and rises just above the Williams, then goes back down again. The road turns to asphalt at the 15 mile mark from Tea Creek, and passes through the community of Dyer, which is a mixture of camp houses and homes hugging the riverbank.

At the 18 mile mark is an interesting grocery, in operation since 1922. You can get something to eat and drink here — you may even want to put together a picnic to eat along the river. Just past the grocery, take a left at the bridge onto FR 101. From here, it's uphill just over 3 miles to the top of Bishop Knob, the only significant climb on the 26 mile route. Approaching Bishop Knob go straight at the first intersection, then stay left until you pass Bishop Knob. After passing the campground, take the third right which is about .6 mile down the road. This will still be FR 101. From here, you have a couple miles to the Cranberry Campground. If you want to have a shuttle waiting for you there, it makes a total trip of 26 miles.

If you are more ambitious, you can continue on the gated road that runs alongside the Cranberry River. FR 101 will turn into FR 76. Eventually FR 76 turns into FR 102. This route will take you on a beautiful ride of about 18 mostly level miles up to the Cranberry Glades boardwalk. At the boardwalk, you can have a shuttle pick you up, or continue out to WV 39/55, where you take a left and go a short distance to the Cranberry Visitor's Center, then left again on the Highland Scenic Highway. It's about 15 hilly but gorgeous miles on the Highway from the Visitor's Center back to Tea Creek.

Where to Stay:

Camping: The Tea Creek Campground and the Day Run Campground are just off Highland Scenic Highway about 15 miles from the Cranberry Visitor's Center. There are a number of good campsites along the Williams River on FR 86 from the Tea Creek Campground.

Bed & Breakfasts: Elk River Inn (304) 572-3771 in Slatyfork. This is part of the Elk River Touring Center, which offer guided bike tours and bike servicing. Other B&B's: Shay Inn (304) 572-3771 in Cass; Jerico B&B (304) 799-6241, The Old Clark Inn (304) 799-6377, Carriage House Inn (304) 799-6706, and The Guest House (304) 799-6711 in or near Marlinton; The Current B&B (304) 653-4722, and Yew Mountain Lodge (304) 653-4821, both near Hillsboro.

5. HOLLY RIVER STATE PARK

The beautiful mountains of Holly River State Park are located in the heart of West Virginia. The park, created in 1938, is about an hour and a half off I-79 at the Flatwoods or Sutton exits.

The history of the area is as interesting as its natural beauty. There is evidence that several American Indian groups camped and hunted around Holly River. The first settlers of European descent moved to the region between 1800 and 1820. Swiss immigrants began to settle here in 1870. The Swiss heritage is preserved in and around the park, particularly in Helvetia, a small community less than 15 miles from Holly River. (*See* Chapter 1, Helvetia.)

The Holly River forests, like many of those in West Virginia, were stripped of timber around the turn of the century. The federal government began to administer the Holly River lands in 1938. Animals were reintroduced, as well as trees such as the Chinese chestnut, autumn olive, mulberry, and hazelnut. Those species, as well as towering hemlocks, pines, and other varieties, cover the hills and hide the scars of past sins.

Holly River State Park is laced with miles of hiking trails that are, unfortunately, off limits to bikers. However, you will find many miles of service roads available for wonderful riding through most areas of the park.

Several 7-8 mile loops exist, or you can make a rough circle around the park that adds up to about 15 miles.

Directions: Holly River is located on WV 20 about 34 miles south of Buckhannon and 22 miles north of Webster Springs. From Charleston, take I-79 North about 65 miles to the Sutton exit. From Sutton, take WV 15 East to WV 20 North. Follow WV 20 North about 10 miles to the park.
 Approaching from I-79 South, take the Buckhannon exit at WV 33 East. From Buckhannon, take WV 20 South to Rock Cave and into Holly River.

KLEE FARM LOOP:
Location: Webster County.
Length: 7.8 miles with shuttle; approximately 9.8 miles without shuttle.
Degree of Difficulty: ***
Scenery: ****
Topo Quads: Hacker Valley and Goshen.
Elevation (in feet): From 1,600 to 2,700.
Footnotes: This is a moderately challenging ride that takes you through peaceful forests and past historic Klee Farm. Using a shuttle will shave about 2 miles of unimproved road from the loop, or you can ride it as a self-contained circle. All mileage is from the trailhead after the shuttle. This trail crosses into private property for about .5 a mile. Check with the park superintendent before riding.

Description: Starting at headquarters just inside the park, either bicycle or shuttle back out to WV 20 and go right. Take another quick right onto Bender Town Rd. You can drive or bike 1 mile or so to a park gate. You'll find a gravel area on the left side of the road across from the gate for parking. At the gate down Bender Town Rd., go right. The trail has a gradual uphill climb, then opens to gentle ups and downs. About .7 mile down this trail, a huge boulder juts out over the road's edge. Just beyond the boulder on the right is a primitive campground, with a picnic table, outhouse, and stone hearth for cooking. Three deer lurched from the spot as I pulled up for a look.

At 2.6 miles from the shuttle drop is a boundary gate that marks the beginning of private property. Although the road re-enters the park after about .5 mile, you should check with the park superintendent about riding on the private road. At about 3.4 miles, follow the road as it cuts sharply to the left and uphill. (On the map this left is shown only as a curve in an otherwise straight trail). A short climb takes you to the top of the hill, and past the old white farmhouse at Klee Farm. This house is still occupied by a descendant of the original Swiss settlers. At Klee Farm, the road goes down to the right, then meets Pickens Rd. at 4.3 miles. Take another right onto the gravel Pickens Rd., and enjoy a 3 mile downhill that dumps you back near park headquarters. The total length of the trip is about 7.8 miles from the gate on Bender Town Rd.

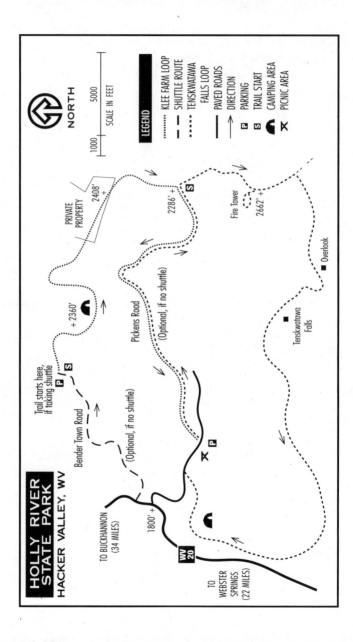

TENSKWATAWA FALLS LOOP:

Location: Webster County.

Length: 6.5 mile loop with shuttle, or about 9.5 miles without.

Degree of Difficulty: ***

Scenery: ****

Topo Quads: Hacker Valley and Goshen.

Elevation (in feet): 1,600 to 3,000.

Footnotes: With the exceptions of a few hills, this is an easy and scenic ride with several overlooks and a waterfall.

Description: This loop takes you around the opposite side of the park. Ride or shuttle several miles uphill from park headquarters on Pickens Rd. to the service road that branches off to the right. I shuttled to the trail, therefore, all mileage references start at the service road. On this trail, you get the hard part out of the way early by heading uphill for about 1 mile. This road goes past an old fire tower that is on the right down a short side trail. Back on the main trail, there is an intersection at about 1.4 miles. Bear right here to keep on the loop. At 2.8 miles, there is an overlook on the left that offers a good view of Potato Knob. Just past the overlook is a foot trail that goes up to an old cemetery where you can see the graves of early settlers. Several headstones and some rocks mark the graves. Look closely at what appears to be a tree stump — it actually is a beautiful cement gravestone. It honors a man named William McClure who died in 1904 at the ripe age of 77.

Back on the trail, at 3.6 miles, you pass Tenskwatawa Falls on the left. This 10 foot waterfall is named after the Indian medicine man, Tenskwatawa. He reportedly demonstrated his powers by darkening the sun at midday near the park on June 16, 1806. At Tenskwatawa Falls, you can walk beneath a massive sandstone outcropping over which the water rushes. It's a great place to rest and cool your head in the water. A second waterfall in the park is named for his brother, Tecumseh. Just past the falls, take the downhill for several miles, which ends at the assistant superintendent's trailer. The total trip with a shuttle is 6.5 miles. By taking a right on the asphalt, you can re-enter the main park area through the campground.

WHERE TO STAY:

Camping: Holly River State Park has an 88 unit campground, a swimming pool, and tennis courts. Cabins can be rented by calling 1-800-CALL-WVA.

NEW RIVER/ GREENBRIER VALLEY

6. New River Gorge
National River

Boulder-lapping white water; rock-faced canyon walls; and trails that weave through lush vegetation and old mining towns all make the New River Gorge National River one of the best playgrounds in West Virginia. The rafting industry has blossomed here in the past decade as the challenges of the New River become more popular. The gorge is also an excellent place for rock climbing, biking, and hiking.

The New River Gorge National River joined the National Park System in 1978. Trails and facilities are still being developed on this 52 mile section of protected river. Although many miles of old logging and mining trails snake through and around the gorge walls, mountain biking hasn't been extensively developed. There are, however, about 20 miles of great trails that offer bicyclists glimpses of the incredible natural beauty and interesting history of the area.

The New River itself is very old, perhaps one of the oldest in the world. The headsprings of the New are in the Blue Ridge Mountains near Boone, North Carolina. The waters gain volume and momentum as they tumble through Virginia into West Virginia, cutting through sandstone, shale, and coal. At some points, the river forms canyons up to 1,300 feet deep and averaging a mile in width.

The completion of the Chesapeake & Ohio Railway

in 1873 opened the gorge to coal companies. Dozens of towns popped up as people moved in to operate the mines. Towns such as Brooklyn, Red Ash, Sewell, Thurmond, and Alaska once thrived, but now are inhabited by only ghosts or mere handfuls of people. The foundations of some of the old homes are still visible beneath vines and brush as you bike the New River trails. In Thurmond, where the movie *Matewan* was filmed, many of the old buildings still stand. There is only one coal mine still operating in the gorge area. However, the entrances to many defunct mines can be seen from the trails.

The New River Gorge Bridge, with the world's longest single arch steel span, rises 876 feet above the gorge. The bridge is the second highest in the United States. On the third Saturday in October, the Fayette County Chamber of Commerce hosts Bridge Day, when visitors can walk the bridge and parachutists can jump from its rails.

Biking in the New River Gorge National River area generally means using a shuttle or out-and-back riding. Considering the scenery, biking twice along the same path isn't bad. Most of the trails now open to biking can be strung together to make one long trip. First I'll describe the trails individually, then mention how they can be connected.

Directions: From I-77 South take the Mossy exit. Go left under the interstate, then right onto Rt. 612. A few miles down Rt. 612 is an intersection. Go straight to reach U.S. 19. From U.S. 19 you are just a couple miles from either end of the gorge trails.

From I-77 North take the Summersville exit on U.S. 19 North for about 5 miles. To reach the Thurmond-Minden Trail, take the Glen Jean exit. The other trails are accessed past Fayetteville just before the New River Gorge Bridge.

THURMOND/MINDEN TRAIL:

Location: Fayette County.
Directions: From U.S. 19 South take the Glen Jean exit on the left at Rt. 25. Rt. 25 will take you into Thurmond. The trailhead parking lot is on the left just before crossing the New River into Thurmond.
Length: Just over 3 miles one way.
Degree of Difficulty: *
Scenery: *****
Topo Quads: Fayetteville and Thurmond.
Elevations (in feet): Minden, 1,600; to a low of 1,120.
Footnotes: This is a delightful and easy ride along a well developed old rail grade — a great trail for the beginning mountain biker.

Description: Start at the trailhead parking area just before Thurmond. There is a gradual climb as the trail heads up to Minden, about 3.2 miles away. Just into the trail, down on the right, you can catch a good view of Thurmond, which edges up to the opposite side of the New River. Proceeding up the trail you come to McKinley Rock, a huge splinter of mountain that separated from the main face and somehow managed to keep from falling into the gorge below. Steps and a boardwalk allow you to continue on the trail between the rock and

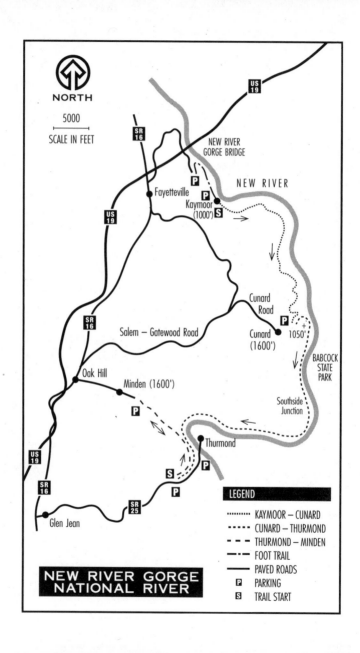

NORTH

5000
SCALE IN FEET

SR 16

NEW RIVER GORGE BRIDGE

NEW RIVER

US 19

Fayetteville

Kaymoor (1000')

Cunard Road

Cunard (1600')

1050'

Salem – Gatewood Road

BABCOCK STATE PARK

SR 16

Oak Hill

Minden (1600')

Southside Junction

Thurmond

US 19

SR 16

SR 25

Glen Jean

LEGEND

········ KAYMOOR – CUNARD
········· CUNARD – THURMOND
– – – – THURMOND – MINDEN
–·–·– FOOT TRAIL
——— PAVED ROADS
P PARKING
S TRAIL START

NEW RIVER GORGE NATIONAL RIVER

the mountain. As you travel to Minden, you'll cross several trestles (park rules ask you to walk your bike here) and wind along Arbuckle Creek. I've biked this trail in spring and summer, and loved it each time. In spring, icicles were still clinging to the mountain face. In summer, rhododendrons bloomed along the trail and in thickets covering the creek below. Once in Minden, you can wander around this sleepy town, or head back down the trail for an easy return.

KAYMOOR TO CUNARD:

Location: Fayette County.

Directions: I started this trail by having someone drop me at the Kaymoor Trail trailhead because of limited parking. From U.S. 19 North from Oak Hill, take the last right before reaching the New River Gorge Bridge. This is Fayette Station Rd. The trailhead is 1 mile or so down on the right. This section of the trail is open only to hikers, but you can walk your bike just about 2 miles and catch some of the area's best views before reaching the Kaymoor mine site. The trails are also accessible by starting at Kaymoor Trailhead parking area on Kaymoor One Rd. To get here take WV 16/61 just north of Oak Hill. Turn right on Salem-Gatewood Rd., and right on Kaymoor One Rd.

Length: 6.8 miles (includes approximately 2 miles of hiking only trail).

Degree of Difficulty: **

Scenery: *****

Topo Quads: Fayetteville and Thurmond.

Elevations (in feet): Start, 1,000; Kaymoor Mine, 1,500; Cunard, 1,600.

Footnotes: If you plan to bike the entire stretch through Cunard and on to Thurmond, it's easier to start from this end. The mileage points listed for these sections of trail are based on starting at Kaymoor Trail.

Description: At 1.5 miles from the Kaymoor Trail trailhead on the right are a couple of abandoned mines. You can walk to the sealed-off mouths of the mines in summer and feel the cool air as it surges from deep underground. At 1.7 and 1.9 miles, check out the views of the gorge to your left and the bridge behind you. The Kaymoor Mine is about 2 miles into the hike. Many of the structures that surrounded this huge mine, which operated from 1899 until 1962, still stand. You start riding your bike at Kaymoor Mine. The trail is narrow in spots, but great fun as you wind along the rim of the gorge, sometimes dipping into the woods. In the summer, listen for the hoots of rafters as they bounce along the river far below. At 3.8 miles is a fork which is not shown on the map. Stay straight rather than take the switchback to the right. At 8.9 miles, you can catch the gravel road at Cunard. There will be a left turn off the trail here that takes you across a wooden foot bridge and up to the gravel road. Take a left here if you want to go downhill to the river and catch the trail over to Thurmond.

CUNARD TO THURMOND (SOUTHSIDE JUNCTION):

Location: Fayette County.

Length: 6 miles.

Degree of Difficulty: **

Scenery: *****

Topo Quads: Fayetteville and Thurmond.

Elevations (in feet): Cunard, 1,600; along the river about 1,050.

Footnotes: If you start this section by exiting the Kaymoor Trail and going downhill on the gravel Cunard Rd., be careful. The road is steep and winding, and in warmer weather there is a regular flow of traffic from rafting outfitters. The trip downhill is just over 1 mile, and you will end up at a boat and raft launching area known as Brooklyn.

Description: Go to the far end of the parking lot and take the gravel road that runs along the river. This road soon becomes unimproved, and may have black, gummy mud pits capable of swallowing a bike. After about 2 miles on this road, the single track trail begins. This is an easy and scenic ride along the river. After 3.3 miles of single track, you'll come to a gravel road. Cross the road where you'll pick up the trail again. Most of the trail on this stretch is hard-packed gravel, with a few roots and rocks. This is an old railroad grade, so look for rail ties that sometimes jut up from the trail. By scanning the brush to your right, you can catch glimpses of the rail towns that once dotted the trail. Crumbling foundations are about all that remain.

About 7 miles from the boat launch at the end of Cunard Rd., you'll reach rail tracks beyond which is a paved road. There is a sign here that says "Southside Junction." You are now just across the bridge from Thurmond. From Southside Junction, you can shuttle out, retrace your tracks and return to your starting point, or head up to the Thurmond/Minden Trail. If you choose the latter, you can reach the trail by walking your bike along the tracks to your right for just over .1 mile. Look for a gravel path going uphill to your right, which climbs gradually for a few tenths of a mile up to Thurmond/Minden. A left here takes you back to the trailhead off Rt. 25. A right takes you to Minden, about 3 miles away. As I mentioned earlier, these trails can be done separately, or strung together to make a trip of over 20 good miles.

MORE BIKING IN THE AREA:

The Ridge Rider Bike Shop, located just off U.S. 19 in Fayetteville, offers rentals, repairs, and tours of the New River Gorge area. ACE Outdoor Center offers guided white water trips, 25 miles of multiple-use trails, and bike rentals. The center, located just outside Minden, has camping facilities and can be used as a starting point for a biking trip. The ACE toll-free number is 1-800-SURF-WVA. For information on similar businesses in the area, call the Fayette County Chamber of Commerce at 1-800-927-0263.

Also, check with the New River Gorge National River headquarters in Glen Jean (304) 465-0508 or the Canyon Rim Visitor's Center at (304) 574-2115 to find out about additions to the bike trail system. A new trail being developed along a rail grade will start where the road crosses the river a couple of miles past the Dun Glen day use area (across the river from Thurmond), and follow the river upstream to somewhere around Terry.

WHERE TO STAY:

Camping: In addition to ACE Outdoor Center, there are several campgrounds in the New River area. Babcock State Park (304) 438-3003, Little Beaver State Park (304) 763-2494, and Summersville Lake (304) 872-3459, all have camping facilities and are within an easy drive of the gorge. Babcock also has lodging facilities.

Bed & Breakfasts: White Horse B&B (304) 574-1400 and The County Seat B&B (304) 574-0823 in Fayetteville.

7. Lake Sherwood Recreation Area

Biking the mountains around beautiful Lake Sherwood in southeastern West Virginia offered the sweet with the sour: panoramic views and thorn-pricked tubes; challenging trails and craggy mountain tops that wouldn't budge. I fought with sections of poor trail, endured cold rain after an Allegheny peak popped open a thunderhead, and fixed five flats on one trip. All this, and I still consider Lake Sherwood a great place to ride.

The recreation area is centered around the 165 acre lake. The lake is cradled in the Allegheny Mountain range near the Virginia border, at 2,700 feet above sea level. Several trails in the recreation area can be tied together with service roads to make loops into the hills. There are also two level trails: one along Meadow Creek, and another that circles the lake. The Blue Bend Recreation Area, although I did not visit it, is just south of Lake Sherwood. A map of the region indicates that several trails from both locations could be pieced together into a decent loop. Check with the national forest district office in White Sulphur Springs for current information. By combining trails around Lake Sherwood, I put together two loops of over 10 miles each.

Directions: Lake Sherwood can be reached by taking WV 92 North from I-64 near the Virginia border. At Neola, turn east onto Rt. 14 and go 11 miles to the Recreation Area.

Loop 1 (Lake Sherwood Trail to Virginia Trail to Allegheny Mountain Trail to Connector Trail to Meadow Creek Trail):

Location: Greenbrier County.

Length: Just over 10 miles.

Degree of Difficulty: ****

Scenery: ****

Topo Quads: Lake Sherwood, Mountain Grove, and Rucker Gap.

Elevations (in feet): Lake, 2,668; Allegheny Mountain Trail, up to 3,200.

Footnotes: Difficulty rating is due to rough going along the Allegheny Mountain Trail, as well as the length of the loop. The scenery is wooded except around the lake. Note that the Allegheny Mountain Trail and the Allegheny Trail are two different trails, as are the Meadow Creek and Meadow Mountain trails. There are some very rocky spots that require carrying your bike.

Description: Park in the picnic area lot on the right just before reaching the guard gate near the lake. Start by going left on the Lake Sherwood Trail (601) for about .6 mile. Just after you cross the spillway bridge, take the Virginia Trail (685) straight ahead. At the 1.1 mile mark watch for a drainage pipe that sticks up from the trail. The Virginia Trail climbs almost 1 mile. At 1.5 miles, take a left on the Allegheny Mountain Trail (611). As you travel this trail, occasionally glance to your right for views of huge Lake Moomaw, spreading out below you in a Virginia valley. An especially good viewing spot is at the 2 mile mark. At 2.2 miles is a fork. (This fork is not shown on the map.) Take the left path, going uphill.

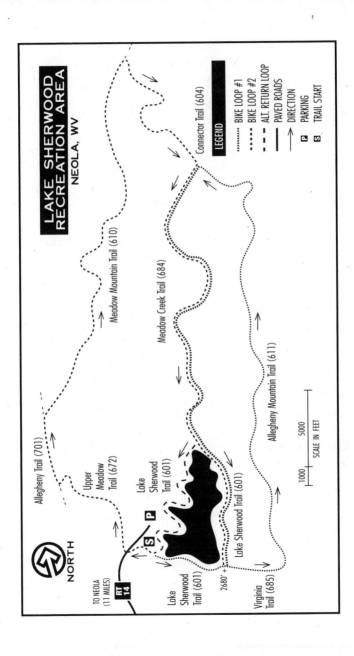

LAKE SHERWOOD RECREATION AREA
NEOLA, WV

NORTH

TO NEOLA
(11 MILES)

RT 14

Allegheny Trail (701)

Upper Meadow Trail (672)

Lake Sherwood Trail (601)

Lake Sherwood Trail (601)

P PARKING

S TRAIL START

2680'+

Virginia Trail (685)

Lake Sherwood Trail (601)

Meadow Mountain Trail (610)

Meadow Creek Trail (684)

Allegheny Mountain Trail (611)

Connector Trail (604)

LEGEND
.... BIKE LOOP #1
.... BIKE LOOP #2
– – – ALT. RETURN LOOP
───── PAVED ROADS
⟶ DIRECTION
P PARKING
S TRAIL START

1000   5000
SCALE IN FEET

You'll get another good view of the lake at 3.3 miles as you cross the ridge. At 3.7 miles, the trail gets narrow and rocky; you might have to push your bike on some stretches. A particularly rough spot begins at 4.2 miles. At 5.3 miles, you catch the Connector Trail (604), which is on your left. At 5.6 miles cross the meadow; the trail picks up on the other side in the right hand corner. At 5.8 miles, up on the left, is the Meadow Creek Trail (684). This trail is mostly level as it follows the creek, but there are also lots of rocks, roots, and creek crossings. At about 8.5 miles, there is an ill-marked left. This left over the creek connects you to the Lake Sherwood Trail. Lake Sherwood Trail will eventually take you across the dam and to the parking lot. At the 8.5 mile mark, I stayed straight, and ended up in the Meadow Creek Campground. Here I caught paved road and took a left back to my car for a total ride of just over 10 miles.

Loop 2 (Upper Meadow Trail to Allegheny Trail to Meadow Mountain Trail to Connector Trail to Meadow Creek Trail):

Length: About 13 miles.
Degree of Difficulty: ****
Scenery: ****
Topo Quads: Lake Sherwood, Mountain Grove, and Rucker Gap.
Elevations (in feet): Meadow Creek Mountain ranges from 3,000 to 3,500.
Footnotes: Difficulty rating reflects climbs, rough riding in spots, and length of trail. The loop wraps around the mountains on the opposite side of Lake Sherwood, and is

slightly longer than the first loop. Again, there were great views, but they were diminished by flat tires and wrong turns at points that weren't marked.

Description: This loop starts at the picnic area, the same as Loop 1, but you go right and take Upper Meadow Trail. The initial section of Upper Meadow Trail (672) crosses the paved road early, then has a few modest climbs before it descends at .8 mile (watch out for a large root). At the bottom of the hill, the trail goes left and becomes part of an old road. At about 1.4 miles, there is a sharp switchback to the left. When I rode the trail, the turn-off wasn't marked and I added several unnecessary miles to my trip on timber-tangled old road. You'll know if you've taken the correct turn by the blue diamond markings on trees. (Check with park personnel to make sure the same markings are still in use.)

Go uphill at the switchback about .1 mile until the intersection with the Allegheny Trail (701). Take a right. Two miles from the start, catch the Meadow Mountain Trail (610) on your right. At 3.2 miles, stay right at the fork. (The fork isn't shown on the map.) Again, the correct trail should be marked with blue diamonds. At 3.6 miles, the road enters a grassy area. Continue through this to the other side, where the road improves, becoming wider and clearer. You begin a downhill here. Beware of ruts caused by drainage ditches — they can send you off your seat.

At 4.2 miles is a gate at an intersection. Go right. (On the map, the area between 4.2 and 5.7 miles is shown as straight. The intersection and FR 311 are not shown.) At 4.6 miles is a fork. Meadow Mountain Trail goes off to the right, while FR 311 continues down to the left. Stay right with the trail for a .3 mile climb to an open, grassy area that affords good views of surrounding valleys. The road here dips for .5 mile. At 5.7 miles on the right you should see a switchback, which is the Connector Trail (604). Take 604 downhill about 1.5 miles, splashing through a creek several times. The trail then goes alongside the creek until you reach the Meadow Creek Trail (684) on your right at 7.3 miles. Go right onto 684. At 10.1 miles, the trail crosses the creek. You can go either way here. A left will put you on the Lake Sherwood Trail, which takes you partially around the impoundment and is a treat to ride. At about 12 miles you will reach the intersection with the Virginia Trail. Take a right and cross the dam. You can also go right at the 10.1 mile mark. This takes a little shortcut back to the car by going around the other side of the lake.

Of Interest in the Area:

For alternatives to biking, lots of water sports are available in and around Lake Sherwood. An option for more hiking or biking is the Greenbrier River Trail, which can be accessed from a number of spots west of Lake Sherwood. From Lake Sherwood you are also within easy reach of the many treasures of Pocahontas County, such as Cass Scenic Railroad, the National Radio Astronomy Observatory in Green Bank, and the Snowshoe/Silver Creek ski area.

WHERE TO STAY:

Camping: There are 96 family units around Lake Sherwood. There are campgrounds and cabins at nearby Watoga State Park and Seneca State Forest, both of which also have biking trails. Call 1-800-CALL-WVA for information, or Seneca Rocks Visitor's Center, at (304) 567-2827.

Bed & Breakfasts and Inns: The Old Clark Inn (304) 799-6377, The Carriage House Inn (304) 799-6706, The Guesthouse (304) 799-7611, and The Jerico B&B (304) 799-6241, in or near Marlinton; The Current B&B (304) 653-4722, and Yew Mountain Lodge (304) 653-4821, both outside Hillsboro; Harris House Lodging (304) 456-4105 and Tranquility B&B (304) 456-3430, in Green Bank.

8. MONCOVE LAKE STATE PARK

Tucked into the southern part of Monroe County is Moncove Lake State Park. The park has a 144 acre lake, surrounded by more then 500 acres of hilly woodland. Swimming, boating, and fishing are all popular on the lake. A large part of the park is open to hunting.

While limited, the trail system at Moncove Lake is fun and enjoyable. It's also convenient if you happen to be in the Greenbrier State Forest, or finishing up the southern stretch of the Greenbrier River Trail. Moncove, a little off the beaten path in Gap Mills, is rural and peaceful. Several trails loop into the hills around the lake, and a couple of service roads offer good out-and-back riding into the woods and along a creek.

Directions: From I-64, take Rt. 311 South on the W.V./Va. border. Follow Rt. 311 South into Virginia. Just after re-entering West Virginia at Sweet Springs, take WV 3 to Gap Mills. Next take a right on Rt. 8 North to the lake. From the interstate, it's about a 30 minute drive to Moncove Lake. Ask park officials for directions for a scenic back road trip from Greenbrier State Forest into the park.

DIAMOND HOLLOW TRAIL:

Location: Monroe County.
Length: Total loop of about 3 miles.
Degree of Difficulty: ***
Scenery: ***
Topo Quad: Paint Bank.
Elevations (in feet): 2,513 to 2,800 feet.
Footnotes: This loop has potential when the brush is cleared and the trails are clearly marked, a job that should be finished by the time of publication of this book. The loop has a mixture of ridgetop views, peaceful woods, and swampy areas, all with plenty of wildlife.

Description: From the road entering Moncove, as you approach the lake, turn left on the road that hugs the lake. Cross the dam and park near the office on the left. Start at Diamond Hollow Trail, which is marked with a sign at the left edge of the campground. The trail climbs about .5 mile, then follows some single track through the woods overlooking the lake. After your initial climb, it becomes rocky. At around 1.1 miles, before a swampy clearing, the trail meets up with Devil's Creek Trail. Here you can stay straight on the main trail, or take a left on Devil's Creek. Devil's Creek Trail goes .65 mile back to the campground. Staying straight on Diamond Hollow, at Devil's Creek you reach a meadow and the creek at 1.25 miles. Here the trail becomes Roxalia Springs Trail, which loops around and ends up at the dam. Go left on the main road at the dam back to the office and campground.

NOTE: *Both Devil's Creek Trail and Roxalia Springs Trail have misleading signs at their entrances near the lake. The*

*signs say "Foot Traffic Only." I was assured by the park
superintendent that bikes are allowed, and that the signs are
to keep out motorized 4-wheelers. Grouse Knoll Trail is the
only trail in Moncove on which bicycles are not allowed.*

COVE CREEK TRAIL:

Location: Monroe County.
Length: Around 3 miles out and back.
Degree of Difficulty: **
Scenery: ****
Topo Quad: Glace.
Elevations (in feet): 2,243 at start to 2,200 at end.
Footnotes: Easy ride, beautiful country scenes.

Description: From the lake, travel northeast on Glace
Rd. (Rt. 8) for about 4 miles, to Cove Creek Rd. on the
right. This gravel road takes you along — and over —
Cove Creek for several miles. It's a beautiful, easy out-
and-back through the woods. Try stopping at one of the
creek crossings to take a cool dip in the water. Like many
streams in West Virginia, Cove Creek waters either rush
over rocks strewn about the stream bed, or race over rocks
layered like a deck of cards. The gentle violence of
geologic change pushes and cajoles the earth into wonderful formations. You'll enjoy the scenery along these roads
and trails.

MIDDLE MOUNTAIN:

Location: Monroe County.
Length: 4 miles out-and-back.

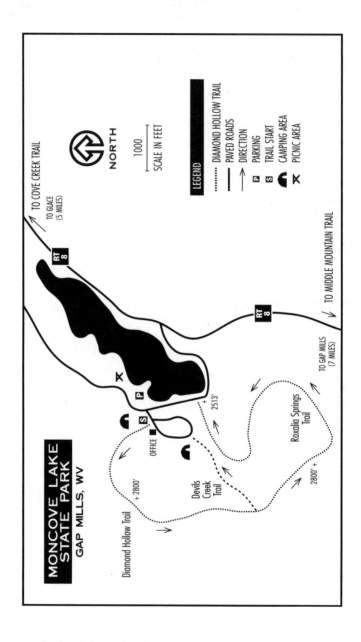

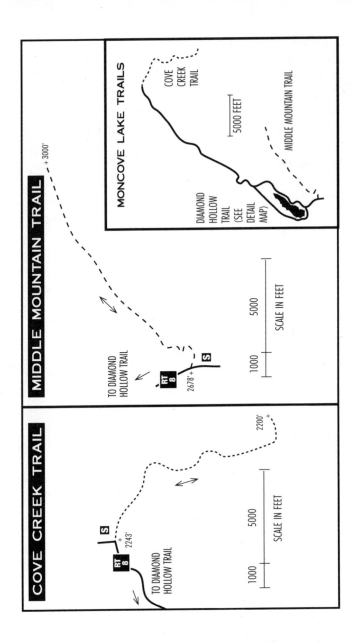

COVE CREEK TRAIL

MIDDLE MOUNTAIN TRAIL

MONCOVE LAKE TRAILS

Degree of Difficulty: ***
Scenery: ***
Topo Quads: Paint Bank and Glace.
Elevations (in feet): 2,678 at start to 3,000 at end.
Footnotes: There is nothing technical about this ride. It is simply a scenic ride into the hills of Monroe County.

Description: Another park service road cuts uphill to the right just before you reach the park entrance off Glace Rd. coming in from Gap Mills. You can park at the orange gate. This road takes you uphill about .5 mile before leveling off into rolling dips along a ridge line. This ride is a total out-and-back of about 4.0 miles. There are no particulars to see on this road, just peaceful woods and the occasional deer, that stops eating long enough to watch you pass.

OF INTEREST IN THE AREA:

In addition to the park, there are several springs in the area that are considered medicinal. Years ago, resorts grew up around these springs. The most famous and luxurious, The Greenbrier, is still very much alive in White Sulphur Springs, about 45 minutes from Moncove Lake. For those interested in spelunking, Organ Cave is about 25 minutes from the park. The historic town of Lewisburg is about 30 minutes away.

WHERE TO STAY:

Camping: There is a 50 site campground at the edge of the lake. Call 1-800 CALL-WVA for reservations.

Bed & Breakfasts: The Sunny Side Tourist Home (304) 722-5756 is in Pickaway in Monroe County; and the Creekside Cottages (304) 832-6430 are near the village of Greenville. There are also plenty of hotels and bed & breakfasts in Lewisburg and White Sulphur Springs.

9. TWIN FALLS RESORT STATE PARK

Twin Falls is a 3,776 acre state park located in Wyoming County, near Mullens. In addition to about 20 miles of hiking and biking trails, the park has an 18-hole golf course, the Pioneer Farm Museum, and a swimming pool. A lodge, cottages, and campsites are available to rent.

Mountains, the highest at 2,409 feet, make the park's topography fairly rugged. While trails often wind up hillsides and along ridges, biking is only moderately difficult. Trails are short — the longest being 4.5 miles — and in good condition. Unlike many parks in the state's system, Twin Falls has opened all its trails to bikers.

The park is about an hour and a half south of Charleston in the middle of coal country. Most of the small towns surrounding Twin Falls grew out of the coal mining industry. Both the people and the economy of Wyoming County reflect their coal mining heritage. This part of Appalachia is not a hotbed of tourism, but I find it fascinating. It harbors a distinct culture with a rich history. The people in the area were amazingly friendly; the scenery and natural beauty were tremendous. Since coal is now mined much more frequently by machines than by men, the economy is searching for new life.

Directions: Twin Falls is southwest of Beckley near Mullens. Take Exit 42 off I-77 and go south on WV 16 for 4.2 miles to the junction with WV 54. Go right, taking WV 54 for 14 miles to Maben, then turn right on WV 97 and go 5.5 miles to a stop sign. Turn left onto Bear Hole Rd. and go about 1 mile to the park.

CLIFFSIDE TRAIL:
Location: Wyoming County.
Length: 4.5 miles out and back.
Degree of Difficulty: ***
Scenery: ****
Topo Quads: McGraws and Mullens.
Elevation (in feet): 2,100 to 2,250.
Footnotes: This loop has a tricky path leading down to the cliffs. It also offers great views. Rappelling is popular in the cliff area, so you may get a chance to observe those crazy sportsmen.

Description: Park at the Bear Wallow Campground, which is on your right past the cottages. Cliffside starts down to the right of the parking lot as a double track, then splits into two single tracks. The trails meet near the edge of a group of cliffs. The right fork takes you down a fairly steep, rocky hill to the Canada Cliffs. You can walk to the cliffs' edge down a short path — a sign marks the way. Take the left fork a short way to reach the Buzzard Cliffs. Both cliffs offer beautiful views of the surrounding hills, with Cabin Creek rushing below in the valley. To return, double back up a hilly, rocky, and rooty ascent that eventually levels out for a nice ride back to Bear Wallow.

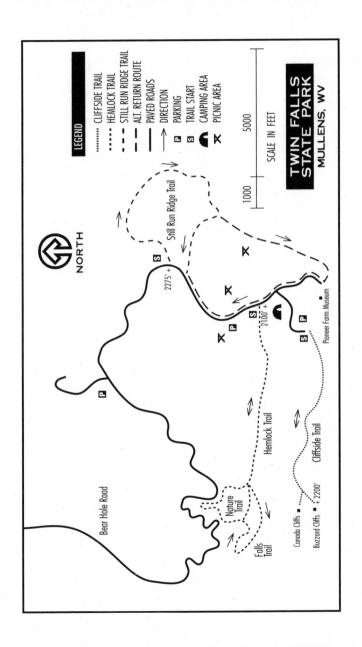

HEMLOCK TRAIL:

Location: Wyoming County.
Length: 4.5 miles out and back.
Degree of Difficulty: **
Scenery: ***
Topo Quads: McGraws and Mullens.
Elevation (in feet): 2,100 to 2,250.
Footnotes: A nice ride through a hemlock forest, with access to other trails that take you to the falls.

Description: Hemlock Trail starts near Cliffside Trail, on the right at Bear Wallow Campground. It is a double track, taking you downhill through hemlock forest and rhododendron thickets. The trail forks into two optional trails at 1 mile. You can double track back to the start with an uphill climb, or hit one of two other trails. You can go left on Falls Trail, and loop for 1.25 miles down around the falls on Marsh Fork and Black Fork. When you hear the roaring water — which roars only during the wet months — stop for a look. Circling about two-thirds of the way around Falls Trail, I caught the Nature Trail on the left. The Nature Trail, a 2 mile single track that edges up to both the highway and the golf course, takes you through a variety of habitats and then back down to Falls Trail. You can then take another left back onto Hemlock Trail to return to the start.

STILL RUN RIDGE TRAIL:

Location: Wyoming County.
Length: 2.5 mile loop, or optional 5-6 mile loop.
Degree of Difficulty: ***

Scenery: ***
Topo Quads: McGraws and Mullens.
Elevation (in feet): 2,275.
Footnotes: This trail offers a quick and relatively easy ride into the woods and past an old hilltop farm.

Description: About 2.5 miles past the cottages on the asphalt road, Still Run Ridge Trail is on your left. Generally level at the start, the trail leads to a fire tower. At about 1 mile into the ride, the trail opens into a grassy meadow highlighted by an old log barn. Just out of the meadow is a downhill ride that starts smooth, but becomes rocky and loose near the bottom. Don't build up too much speed — a fellow rider ended up scooting down the hill on his backside, with his bike in hot pursuit. The last .5 mile is a steep climb. Still Run intersects with a boundary road. If you want an option to finishing the trail in a nearby ball field, take the boundary road to the left. After about 2 miles along a forested road, catch the Huckleberry Trail to your right. It winds through a pine thicket and dumps you down near the Pioneer Farm Museum, which offers a look at life in early Wyoming County. A short ride up the asphalt takes you back to Bear Wallow for about a 5 mile ride.

MORE RIDING IN THE AREA:

Several other smaller trails wind through the park, but are better for hiking than biking. Also snaking through the entire region are numerous gas company and logging roads. Locals say these roads offer great riding and vastly

extended trails. Efforts are being made to designate public access to some of these roads. At this time however, check with park management to find out about access. If public access is granted on these roads, the mountain biking potential for this area will be virtually unlimited.

WHERE TO STAY:

Camping: A campground, lodge and cabins are available within the park. Reservations can be made by calling 1-800-CALL-WVA.

10. PIPESTEM RESORT STATE PARK

Panoramic vistas, the gentle Bluestone River, and an abundance of wildlife, all make Pipestem Resort State Park a favorite in the West Virginia park system. The 4,000 acre park includes an expansive plateau, the 1,000 foot deep Bluestone Canyon, and stacks of mountain ridges. Pipestem, sitting in southern West Virginia less than two hours from Charleston, got its name from a woody shrub whose stem was used in earlier times for making pipes.

Pipestem is designated a "resort park" because it has golf courses, swimming pools, and two lodges. However, it also offers plenty of standard camping facilities, along with ample opportunities to hike and bike. Currently, only 5 of the 16 trails in the park are open to mountain bikes, but 2 good trips can be arranged by combining the trails. One trip takes you around a peaceful lake. The other goes down to the river at the bottom of Bluestone Canyon and up the other side of the canyon wall.

Directions: Pipestem is 20 miles north of Princeton and 12 miles south of Hinton on WV 20. From I-77, take Exit 14, the Athens Rd. exit, near the W.V./Va. border. From here, it's 14 miles to the park. Pipestem can also be reached by taking I-64 to the Sandstone exit east of Beckley, then traveling 22 miles south on WV 20.

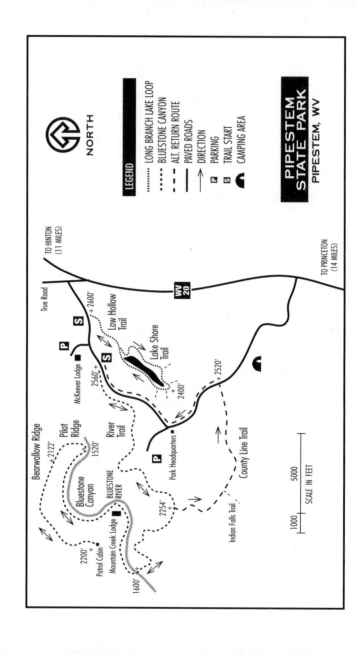

Long Branch Lake Loop:

Location: Summers County.
Length: About 3 miles.
Degree of Difficulty: ***
Scenery: ****
Topo Quad: Pipestem.
Elevations (in feet): Between 2,400 and 2,600.
Footnotes: Warm up for a longer ride, see the lake and the woods, and enjoy Pipestem. Keep an eye out for hikers, fishermen, and people on horseback. If you begin your ride at the campground, you can add another 6 miles or so onto the trip.

Description: From park headquarters go past McKeever Lodge and the golf course toward True Rd. Less than .5 mile past the lodge you'll see Law Hollow Trail on the right. Law Hollow takes you down an old logging road .7 mile to Long Branch Lake. Go left here to catch the Lake Shore Trail, which circles the lake. Stay right on the 3 or 4 offshoots off Lake Shore Trail, to loop around the lake. A brief uphill climb gets you to a mostly level trail. At 1.7 miles, the trail dips down to the edge of the lake, where I stopped for a quiet break. The trail goes back up into the woods, then follows a nice path back along the lake to rejoin Law Hollow. Go left at Law Hollow to the pavement, for a total ride of about 3 miles. The ride around the lake is fun, and the trail is well-maintained.

BLUESTONE CANYON TRAIL:

Location: Summers County.

Length: About 15 miles out-and-back.

Degree of Difficulty: ****

Scenery: *****

Topo Quads: Flat Top and Pipestem.

Elevation (in feet): From 2,560 at the start; to 1,600 at Bluestone River; to 2,200 at the patrol cabin.

Footnotes: The difficulty rating is based on the length and long climbs on either side of the Bluestone River. Travel with a good amount of water and a snack, and enjoy a beautiful ride into the gorge. The River Trail is a longer and more demanding ride than Long Branch Lake Loop, but offers plenty of rewards for the effort.

Description: Starting at park headquarters and just before reaching McKeever Lodge, go left on the River Trail. The trip down to Bluestone River is a winding 3.2 miles. This is a great downhill, but watch your speed — some spots offer little margin for error. Be careful: at one point there is a rock wall on your left and a steep drop-off on your right, neither of which are inviting for a run away bike. After arriving at Bluestone River, there is a sharp right and then a .1 mile stretch that takes you to the river crossing. A sign just before the crossing says that the river in normal conditions is about 18 inches deep, and warns of more dangerous water after heavy rains. When I crossed, it didn't go past my knees. Rather than carry the bike, which makes it hard to balance on moss-covered rocks, I rolled it along the river bottom. The rocky shore on the other side of the river is a good place to stop and take in the beauty of Bluestone Gorge. Tree-shrouded mountains line either side of the water, and exposed rocks jut out from the forests on the left.

Travel up from the shore a few yards, then take a right on the service road, which takes you along the river past the Mountain Creek Lodge less than 1 mile away. At 5.1 miles there is a fork. The two paths rejoin; however, only the one on the left is marked. Go left at another fork at 5.2 miles. The trail narrows, starts up Pilot Ridge, and the going gets considerably more difficult. At about the 6 mile mark, on a little rise to the right, is a small cemetery. You can see the top of one headstone from the trail. Most of the markers are only flat stones stuck into the ground, but several have names and dates.

Continuing up the trail will take you to the patrol cabin. At the patrol cabin, take a breather, then turn around. The ride back down to the river is fast and fun. Retrace the route back past the Mountain Creek Lodge and across the river, then head back uphill.

One option to puffing your way out of the gorge along the River Trail is to take the County Line Trail. This trail begins after you've re-crossed the river and traveled about 1 mile back up the River Trail. It is on the right, and offers a much easier ride than the River Trail. Along this trail you can see signs of early settlers, such as old split-rail fencing and clearings. On the right at .7 mile is Indian Falls. Don't try to ride your bike down the short trail to the overlook. There is a steep cliff at the trail's abrupt end that could easily spell doom. The last .3 mile on the trail is steep and rocky in places, but most of it's fun. At 2 miles from where you turned off the River Trail, you reach the Nature Center, which sits just off the main park road. A left here will return you to park headquarters. You'll have about a 15 mile round trip on scenic and sometimes challenging trails.

Of Interest in the Area:

Pipestem is a self-contained park, with all the amenities necessary for a comfortable stay. The Oak Tree Restaurant, just outside the park entrance, offers an alternative to the park eateries. Just north of Pipestem on WV 20 are Bluestone Lake and Bluestone State Park. Beyond that, also on WV 20 past Hinton, is the beautiful Sandstone Falls.

Where to Stay:

Camping: There is an 82 site campground, two lodges and cabins for rent within the park. Call 1-800-CALL-WVA for reservations.

11. THE GREENBRIER RIVER TRAIL

This rail trail is the jewel in the system of rail trails developed by the state. It is almost 80 miles long, level, and parallels the beautiful Greenbrier River. The river and trail travel through forests and past small communities and farms. The trail runs from Cass in the north to Caldwell in the south. The ambitious biker can ride from one end to the other, camping along the way.

Those who want a rail trail "sampler" can start at one of the access points and travel to another spot to meet a shuttle. I've biked both ends of the trail, but not much of the middle. On the northern end are several remarkably beautiful stretches. The southern end is equally beautiful, but a little more mellow. One of my favorite rides was from Clover Lick, through Stony Bottom, and up to Cass. This 10 mile section takes you through small communities and alongside some great spots for fishing, swimming, or rock-sitting. The last mile of rail line into Cass is still in place and can't be ridden, but you can reach Cass by taking a couple of country roads. This town is worth a visit, or even an overnight stay. You'll find interesting sites and accommodations, such as the old steam engines that take tourists up past abandoned timber towns; and a small hotel in Stony Bottom, which is a nice, quiet place to relax and enjoy the country.

Following is a summary of trail highlights provided by the State Division of Tourism and Parks. Please note on the map that after each small town I have added the number of the (closest) mile marker.

GREENBRIER RIVER TRAIL, NORTH CALDWELL TO CASS:

Location: Greenbrier and Pocahontas Counties.
Length: 80 miles.
Degree of Difficulty: *
Scenery: **** to *****
Topo Quads: not needed.
Elevations (in feet): Caldwell, 1,700; Cass, 2,452.
Footnotes: As a general rule, north to south biking is easier, but the grade is so small that biking is easy on any part of the trail. Difficulty increases only with greater distances.

North Caldwell to Horrock:

Mile Post 3: Trailhead - 1.3 miles north of U.S. 60 at Caldwell on Rt. 38 (Stonehouse Rd.). Parking area, picnic tables, groceries, post office, and public phone at Caldwell. Camping available nearby at Greenbrier State Forest.

Mile 4.7: Campsite - Table, fire ring, no facilities.

Mile 5.8: Harper - (Hopper) From Rt. 38, take Rt. 30/3.

Mile 11.1: Keister - From Rt. 38, take Rt. 30 to Rt. 21 and Rt. 30/1.

Mile 13.5: Campsite - Table, fire ring, no facilities.

Mile Post 14: Anthony - From U.S. 219 at Frankford, 4.9 miles on Rt. 21 and Rt. 21/2. Parking beside trail. Groceries, post office, public phone at Frankford.

Mile 21.5: Spring Creek - From U.S. 219, 1.5 miles north of Frankford, east 3.5 miles on Route 13.

Mile 24.5: Renick - From U.S. 219, east .4 miles on Rt. 11. Parking beside trail. Groceries, post office, public phone along U.S. 219.

Mile 28.5: Campsite - Table, fire ring, no facilities.

Mile 29.6: Horrock - From U.S. 219, east 4.1 miles on Rt. 7 (Brownstown Rd.), then 1.2 miles on Rt. 7/1 to Rt. 7/2, .5 mile to trail.

Horrock to Seebert:

Mile 30.9: Horrock - Droop Mountain Tunnel (402 feet). Trail access point, parking.

Mile 32.3: Campsite - East side of trail, no water.

Mile 33.7: Campsite - East side of trail, unapproved spring on west side of trail at 33.6.

Mile 38.5: Beard - Trail access point, parking, nearby bed and breakfast.

Mile 39.3: Denmar - Trail access point, parking.

Mile 40.9: Campsite - West of trail, no water.

Mile 41.7: Burnside - Trail access point, parking.

Mile Post 44: Fee camping at Watoga State Park Riverside Campground (east side of river).

Mile 45.8: Seebert - Trail access point, parking, cabins (by reservation), camping, meals, drinking water, and public phone available at Watoga State Park. Call 1-800 CALL-WVA for reservations.

Seebert to Marlinton:

Mile Post 46: Several access points and parking.

Mile Post 47: Rt. 219 access point and parking.

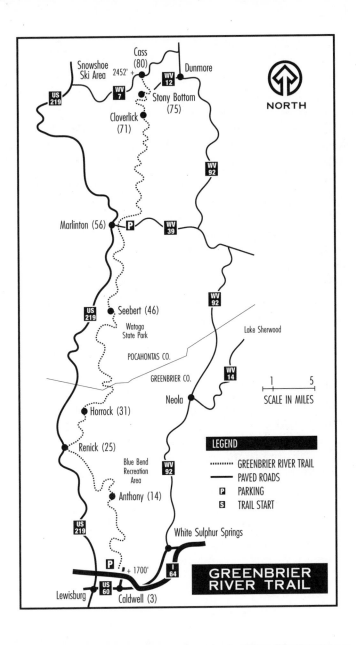

NORTH

Snowshoe Ski Area

Cass (80)

Dunmore

2452'

WV 7

WV 12

Stony Bottom (75)

Cloverlick (71)

US 219

WV 92

Marlinton (56)

P

WV 39

Seebert (46)

US 219

Watoga State Park

Lake Sherwood

POCAHONTAS CO.

GREENBRIER CO.

WV 14

Neola

1   5
SCALE IN MILES

Horrock (31)

Renick (25)

Blue Bend Recreation Area

WV 92

LEGEND

··········· GREENBRIER RIVER TRAIL

———— PAVED ROADS

P   PARKING

S   TRAIL START

Anthony (14)

US 219

White Sulphur Springs

P   + 1700'

I 64

US 60

Lewisburg

Caldwell (3)

GREENBRIER RIVER TRAIL

Mile 47.9: Watoga Bridge - Trail access to east side of Greenbrier River.

Mile 48.1: Site of old town of Watoga - Remnants of bank safe may be seen east of trail.

Mile 49.3: Mouth of Beaver Creek Campsite.

Mile 52.1: Buckeye - Trail access and parking.

Mile 55.1: Stillwell Park Campsite.

Mile 55.8: Knapp's Creek Bridge.

Mile Post 56: Marlinton - Parking, phone, meals, lodging, post office, drinking water, hospital.

Marlinton to Clover Lick:

Mile 56.1: Marlinton - Trail access point, groceries, information depot. Depot was completed in 1901.

Mile 56.5: Only remaining water tank on GRT, built in 1923. Water intake and cement pump house are along river bank at 56.7.

Mile 63.7: Campsite - East side of trail.

Mile 65.7: Sharp's Tunnel and bridge, built in 1900. Tunnel is 511 feet long and bridge is 229 feet long.

Mile 69.6: Campsite - East side of trail.

Mile 70.3: A grease reservoir on the west side of the trail is all that remains of an automatic greasing system. This system reduced friction between the wheel flanges and rails as the train rounded this curve.

Mile 71.1: Clover Lick - Trail access point, parking. Old bridge piers provided rail service to Raine Lumber Company band mill on east side of river, 1913-1929. C&O Depot was moved to private property about 100 yards up the back mountain road toward Marlinton (Depot is on right).

Clover Lick to Cass:
Mile 74.5: Stony Bottom - Trail access point. Lodging and public phone.
Mile Post 77: Sitlington - Access point to trail. Limited parking. First access point below Cass suitable for bicycle access.
Mile Post 80: Cass - Trail access point. Lodging, public phone, food, post office, gift shops, first aid, drinking water, parking, groceries.

*NOTE: For more detailed information on the Greenbrier River Trail, I recommend Jim Hudson's, **The Greenbrier River and West Fork Rail Trails**.*

WHERE TO STAY:

There are numerous hotels, bed & breakfasts, and campsites in towns near the trail. Lewisburg, Marlinton, and Cass are the major towns. State forest and campsites dot the area as well. Call 1-800-CALL-WVA for specific information.

12. Greenbrier State Forest

The trail system at Greenbrier State Forest, like those at several other state forests and parks, is constantly being upgraded. Loops in the forest offer bicyclists access to a variety of areas between the main park road and the county road that bisects the forest. Most of the trails take riders up and across the face of Kate's Mountain. The trails are generally single track, with moderate to steep climbs. There are currently 9.2 miles of biking trails in the forest. The entrance to the forest is only a few miles from the lower end of the Greenbrier River Trail. The forest would be a good side trip before or after the river trail. I rode sections of trails that were under development in the summer of 1994, but I couldn't complete any of the trails. I later called and got descriptions of the new trails from Assistant Superintendent Sam England. Since I didn't ride the completed trails, they aren't rated. However, three trails are described below. Elevations range from 1,826 to 3,161 feet. Topo quads are Glace and White Sulphur Springs.

Directions: Greenbrier State Forest is located in Caldwell, just off I-64. From Lewisburg on I-64 East, take the White Sulphur Springs exit and go right on Rt. 14 for about 1 mile.

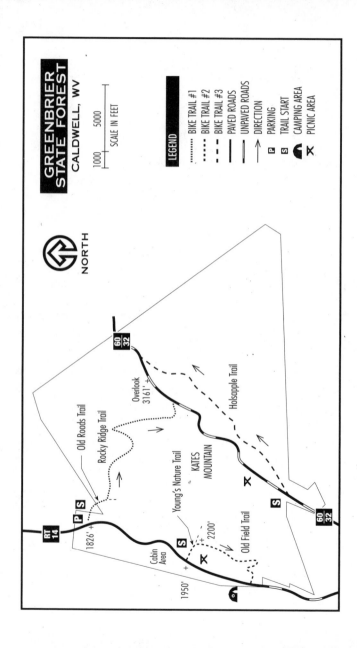

TRAIL ONE:

This trail is off the Old Roads Trail, accessed from behind the service area, which is behind the pool area. Take Old Roads Trail to Rocky Ridge Trail on your left. At about the 1 mile point on the left is a clearing. This is just before Rocky Ridge gets steep. A left at the clearing takes you into about 3-4 miles of old logging roads north of Rocky Ridge on Rt. 60/32.

TRAIL TWO:

Start this trail at the trailhead to Young's Nature Trail, which is just past the cabin area on the left. Go a short bit up Young's Nature Trail until you see a sign for the Old Field Trail on your right. This 1.5 mile trail goes south and then dips back down to the main forest road.

TRAIL THREE:

The Holsapple Trail is in the back of the forest. Take Rt. 60/14 to the intersection with Rt. 60/32. Take a left on this road and go up Kate's Mountain. Once on the mountain, look for the Holsapple sign on the right. The trail is a moderate ride on an old logging road that parallels Rt. 60/32 for 2.2 miles.

WHERE TO STAY:

Camping: Facilities at the forest include a dozen standard cabins, a campground, picnic shelters, and a swimming pool. Call 1-800-CALL-WVA for more information.

Bed & Breakfasts and Inns: General Lewis Inn (304) 645-2600, Oak Knoll B&B (304) 392-6903, and Minnie Manor (304) 647-4096, in Lewisburg; James Wylie House B&B (304) 536-9444, in White Sulphur Springs.

13. CAMP CREEK STATE PARK AND STATE FOREST

Just beyond the hum of cars and the snort of tractor trailers along the West Virginia Turnpike are Camp Creek State Park and Camp Creek State Forest. The park is about 500 acres and the adjacent forest is 5,300 acres. Both are located in Mercer County about an hour and a half south of Charleston.

The best biking in Camp Creek is among the large network of gas well and logging roads that meander through the forest. A total of about 60 miles of roads and trails are open for biking. The road system is not well documented on park maps, and new roads are occasionally opened. Therefore, Camp Creek can be a different adventure each time you ride. I biked the forest roads in May, when spring wildflowers were everywhere.

The roads through Camp Creek can be frustrating or challenging, depending on your attitude. Some disappear into the woods, while others wrap around ridges to join new passageways through the forest. The roads traveled regularly are clear of brush. Many of the older trails are at times reduced to single track. Some may not be worth the effort due to lots of fallen timber. Large, fist-sized rocks are used to fix bad spots in the road, and offer all the pleasure of riding a jackhammer as you bounce over them. Overall, however, Camp Creek offers plenty of great riding. Although I didn't explore all the roads, I discovered several main arteries that offer access to the inner forest.

Directions: Camp Creek is off I-77 about 18 miles south of Beckley at Exit 20 (there are signs for the forest). From I-77 South, go right off the exit and travel 100 yards. Next go right again and follow a two lane paved road for about 2 miles into the forest.

FARLEY KNOB:

Location: Mercer County.
Length: About 7 miles out-and-back; side roads offer some variations.
Degree of Difficulty: ***
Scenery: ***
Topo Quads: Odd and Flat Top.
Elevation (in feet): 2,100 to 2,750.
Footnotes: Difficulty rating is based on steep initial climb. This rating could change, depending on side trails.

Description: Veer right off the main road past the superintendent's office and head to the Blue Jay Campground. At the campground, take the gravel road straight ahead, which is level for about 1 mile. You can park at the end of the road. The trail travels beside Camp Creek and past a beautiful waterfall, before heading up a steep hill. The ascent is about .8 mile. The road forks at the top of the ridge. The left fork takes you west toward a ridge that is easy riding. I rode the left fork for about 2 miles, past a gas compressor and gas well, before the road disappeared into a tangle of brush. There are a number of roads leading off this one that offer side trips of varying distances.

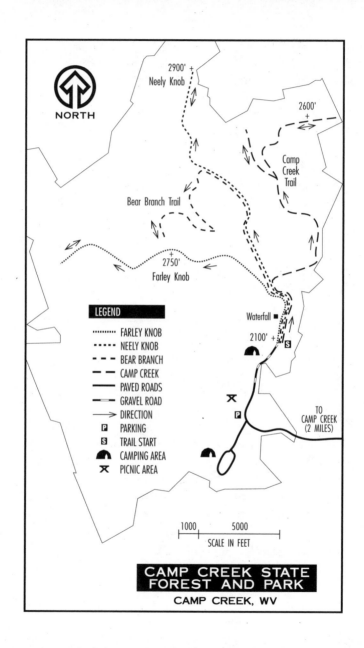

NORTH

2900' +
Neely Knob

2600'
+

Camp
Creek
Trail

Bear Branch Trail

+
2750'
Farley Knob

Waterfall ■

2100' +

S

LEGEND

.... FARLEY KNOB
•••••• NEELY KNOB
------ BEAR BRANCH
— — CAMP CREEK
——— PAVED ROADS
▭ GRAVEL ROAD
→ DIRECTION
P PARKING
S TRAIL START
⛺ CAMPING AREA
✗ PICNIC AREA

✗

P

TO
CAMP CREEK
(2 MILES)

1000   5000
SCALE IN FEET

CAMP CREEK STATE
FOREST AND PARK

CAMP CREEK, WV

NEELY KNOB:

Location: Mercer County.
Length: About 5.4 miles out-and-back.
Degree of Difficulty: ****
Scenery: ***
Topo Quads: Odd and Flat Top.
Elevation (in feet): 2,100 to 2,900 at Neely Knob.
Footnotes: The early climbs make this a challenging ride, but the path is clear and not difficult to follow. There are several nice views along the way, especially at the end. Mileage given is from the turnoff at Blue Jay Campground.

Description: Take the same road as Farley Knob (above) past Blue Jay, but turn right and cross the bridge over the creek before the road starts to climb. Several 100 yards later, another road forks off to the left. At this left, a 1.3 mile uphill awaits you. At 1.5 miles from Blue Jay is a fork. The road to the right follows a ridge out to Neely Knob. At 2.7 miles, you'll hit an iron gate (hopefully not in a literal way) that marks the forest boundary. From here you'll have a beautiful view of the surrounding mountains. Just beyond the boundary gate is a logging road that looks inviting, but unfortunately meanders through private property. I turned around here and had an easy downhill back.

BEAR BRANCH TRAIL (OFFSHOOT OF NEELY KNOB):

Location: Mercer County.
Length: About 5.5 miles out-and-back.
Degree of Difficulty: ****

Scenery: ***
Topo Quads: Odd and Flat Top.
Elevation (in feet): 2,100 to 2,650.
Footnotes: This area of the forest is laced with roads and old trails. Check with park officials to see whether any new maps are available that show all the service roads.

Description: By taking the left instead of the right fork at 1.5 miles into the Neely Knob Route (above), you go deep into the hills. This road has lots of branches, and connects to a number of other trails. There are many options for those who want to explore. I rode 1 mile or so along this road before being forced to turn around due to fallen trees. Park machinery was in the area, so I assume the roads were being cleared.

Camp Creek Trail:
Location: Mercer County.
Length: 6-7 miles out-and-back.
Degree of Difficulty: **
Scenery: ***
Topo Quads: Odd and Flat Top.
Elevation (in feet): 2,100 to 2,600.
Footnotes: This is a generally level ride.

Description: Follow the road past Blue Jay. Take the right that leads to the turnoff for Neely Knob and Bear Branch, but stay straight on that road. You'll have to carry your bike over Camp Creek at about 1 mile down the road. The trail on the other side runs parallel to the creek, passing through swampy areas and briefly over the bed of an old rail line. The road is level, and with a little work could be an excellent biking path. Just under 2 miles into the trail is a fork. Going left for a short distance takes you to a creek. Going right at the fork takes you further toward the forest boundary, several miles away. Thick, downed trees forced me stop again. Turn around to return to Blue Jay Campground.

WHERE TO STAY:

Camping: In addition to recreation and picnic areas for day use, there are two campgrounds — one with 25 trailer hookups, electricity and bathhouse, and the other with 12 rustic sites along Camp Creek. For reservations call 1-800-CALL-WVA.

METRO VALLEY

14. Kanawha State Forest

14. KANAWHA STATE FOREST

Just minutes from Charleston, Kanawha State Forest offers a great escape for weary urbanites and energetic mountain bikers. The 9,300 acre forest is etched with 30 miles of great biking trails that take you to rocky overlooks, abandoned coal mines, and majestic ridges. The forest has campsites, a swimming pool, and horseback riding. Call (304) 346-5654 for information on reservations, seasons, and hours.

Riding a combination of single track and service roads is the norm in Kanawha State Forest. I tend to use the service roads that weave across ridges as dumping off points for the steeper, more challenging trails. Get a forest map and mix your own loops for variety. Not all trails are open to bikers — these are generally marked at the trailhead. You can also check these trails on a trail guide obtained from a box at the front office.

Directions: From Charleston, take U.S. 119 (Corridor G) about 1 mile south toward Logan. Take a left at the light at Oakwood Rd.; follow the signs to the forest. Oakwood Rd. bears to the left and ends at Bridge Rd. Go right on Bridge Rd., follow its curves, then go right again on Connell Rd. (you'll see signs.) At the end of Connell Rd., take a hard left on Loudendale Rd., which takes you to Kanawha State Forest.

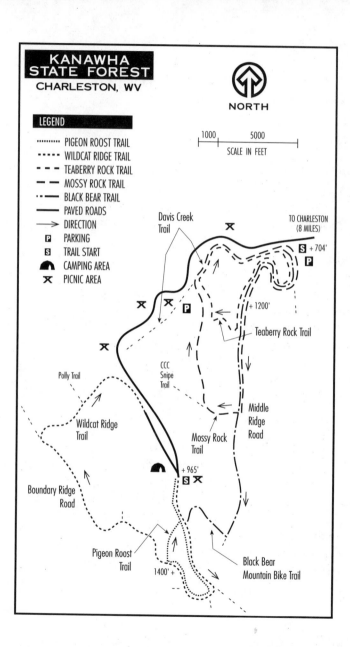

PIGEON ROOST TRAIL

Location: Kanawha County.
Length: 4 miles.
Degree of Difficulty: ***
Scenery: ***
Topo Quads: Charleston West and Racine.
Elevation (in feet): From 965 to over 1,400.
Footnotes: Once up the initial hill, this is a relatively easy ride with a fun descent through the woods.

Description: Take the road into Kanawha State Forest for several miles until the pavement ends at the picnic and parking area. At the parking area, begin biking on the gravel road. It goes gradually uphill from .4 mile to 1.5 miles, where you go right up a steeper, dirt road. Once you get to the top of this boundary road, it's pretty gentle, with just a few ruts and hills. At about 3.3 miles, you'll see a sign for Pigeon Roost Trail on your right. This .75 mile single track takes you back to the gravel road where you started, just down from the picnic and parking area. The trail has a few tricky hills and rocky switchbacks, but generally is fun riding. Beware of the ditch at the bottom of the hill alongside the gravel road. I saw a biker sprawled on the road after the ditch rudely divorced him from his bike.

WILDCAT RIDGE TRAIL

Location: Kanawha County.
Length: 9 miles.
Degree of Difficulty: ****
Scenery: ***

Topo Quads: Charleston West and Racine.
Elevation (in feet): 965 to over 1,400.
Footnotes: The difficulty rating is based on distance and a steep plunge off a ridge to get back to level ground. If you are good on hills, go for it. Wildcat Ridge Trail is a more challenging single track than Pigeon Roost Trail.

Description: Park and follow the same directions as for Pigeon Roost Trail (above). On Boundary Ridge Road, go straight at Pigeon Roost. At 3.9 miles, take a left down a rougher road that plunges into the woods. At 5.5 miles go right on Wildcat Ridge Trail. Wildcat Ridge goes along a ridge for 1 mile or so, then starts downhill. At this point, Polly Trail appears on the left. Keep straight.

There are plenty of tricky spots here. If you're not good at negotiating curves at a steady speed, be careful. One turn in particular edges up to an abrupt drop-off, which lies in wait for bikers who can't quite cut the curve. At 7.1 miles take a sharp right. At the edge of the curve watch for a gaping hole left by an uprooted tree. Just past the curve is a fork. The left fork is more mellow, but with switchbacks. The right fork is straight downhill. If you choose the steeper version, sit far back on your seat and keep your fingers near the brakes. An improperly taken stone or root can catapult you into the woods. Believe me, I know.

You reach the bottom at 7.3 miles. Take a right here and a trail will lead you past a field and into the woods for a short distance. You end up on an asphalt road in the campground. Continue on this road and you'll hit the main forest road, just up from the picnic area where you parked. The total distance of the loop is about 9 miles.

TEABERRY ROCK:

Location: Kanawha County.
Length: About 4.5 miles.
Degree of Difficulty: ***
Scenery: ***
Topo Quads: Charleston West and Racine.
Elevation (in feet): 704 to over 1,200.
Footnotes: Be prepared for a good climb to reach Middle Ridge.

Description: Pigeon Roost and Wildcat Ridge are on the right hand side as you enter the forest. To access the loops on the left hand side, take Middle Ridge Road. One point of access for Middle Ridge is near the entrance gate. You can park in the gravel lot on the left before entering the forest. Follow the gravel road to the left of the entrance for .5 mile toward the shooting range. On your right at .5 mile is Middle Ridge, a gated road that heads uphill. You'll climb about 1.5 miles before the road levels on a ridge. At 2.2 miles is Teaberry Rock, which is off to the right just beyond a gas well. After you've gone into the woods a short distance, look for a side trail that goes into the brush on your left. There is a nice overlook just off this trail, which soon rejoins the main trail. Teaberry Rock dips and dives through the woods for a mile or so before hitting Davis Creek Trail. You can take a right on this trail and follow Davis Creek back to the forest entrance just over 1 mile away.

Mossy Rock Trail:

Location: Kanawha County.
Length: 6.4 miles.
Degree of Difficulty: ***
Scenery: ***
Topo Quads: Charleston West and Racine.
Elevation (in feet): 704 to 1,200.
Footnotes: This is a good workout with a fun downhill and a pleasant ride along Davis Creek.

Description: To make this loop, begin as you would on Teaberry Rock Trail (above), but continue on Middle Ridge to Mossy Rock Trail, at 3.2 miles from the park entrance. Take a right here into the woods. At the 4 mile mark is the CCC Snipe Trail, which is off limits to bikers. Instead, go right on the service road that intersects the trail here, and go downhill just over 1 mile. At 5.1 miles go right on Davis Creek Trail, which leads you back to the forest entrance, for a total ride of 6.4 miles.

Black Bear Trail:

Location: Kanawha County.
Length: About 6 miles down to the main road at the lower end of the forest, or over 9 miles back to the forest entrance.
Degree of Difficulty: *****
Scenery: ***
Topo Quads: Charleston West and Racine.
Elevation (in feet): 704 to over 1,200.
Footnotes: Beware of Black Bear! The difficulty rating is based on the extreme technical challenge of Black Bear Trail.

Description: Another option off Middle Ridge is to begin as you did on Teaberry and Mossy Rock (above), but continue past Mossy Rock a couple miles until you reach Black Bear Trail on the right. This trail is truly meant for sturdy mountain bikes and experienced riders. Black Bear is rock-studded and root-veined, with enough steep plunges and tight turns to hold any biker's attention. If you can endure this treatment for .5 mile, you will find yourself back on the main road that bisects the forest. Take a right on the gravel road, which soon turns into asphalt, if you want to return to the entrance over 3 miles away.

If you want to avoid the asphalt, cut through the campground on the left just after you hit the paved road in the picnic area. At the far end of the camping area, take the gravel road through the woods for a short distance, then past some open meadows. Continue on the gravel road past some small picnic areas until you again hit the paved road. Travel up to the picnic area on the right across from Polly Hollow, then catch the Davis Creek Trail, which runs parallel to the main forest road.

An alternative to heading back to the forest entrance is to go left on the gravel road after you get off Black Bear. This will take you to the boundary road on the right side of the forest, (described in Pigeon Roost and Wildcat Ridge Trails) giving you a longer ride.

MORE RIDING IN THE AREA:

There are other roads and trails that can take you further into the forest for longer and more demanding rides. Check with the forest office (304) 346-5654, and local bike shops and clubs for updated trail and mountain bike race information.

The Black Bear 40-K Mountain Bike Race takes place on the first weekend in August in Kanawha State Forest. Sponsored by Mountain State Bicycles of Teays Valley, the race serves as a benefit for the Forest. *Black Bear* draws about 200 racers from West Virginia and the region. This race was voted one of the Top 10 Mountain Bike Races in the Midwest by *Bike Midwest Magazine* in 1994. With one of the steepest descents in the East and four grueling climbs, the 25-mile *Black Bear* is a must for mountain bike racers from all over. For more information, contact Race Director Robin Brown Broughton at: Mountain State Bicycles, 107 Liberty Square, Hurricane, WV 25526, (304) 757-0308. See Appendix 2 for more information.

WHERE TO STAY:

Camping and Lodging: There is a campground in the forest. For reservations call (304) 346-5654. A large selection of lodging facilities is available 15 minutes away in Charleston.

MID–OHIO VALLEY

154   *Charles Fork Lake*

15. Charles Fork Lake, Spencer

Charles Fork Lake Trails:
Location: Spencer, Roane County.

Directions: From Charleston, take I-79 North for 20 miles to the Clendenin exit. Take U.S. 119 North about 25 miles to Spencer. Entering Spencer, take a right on Rt. 36 across a small bridge. About 1 mile down Rt. 36, there is a dirt road on the right, beyond which are a bridge and a farmhouse. Go right on the dirt road for 1 mile or so, and you'll see a picnic area and a small cabin on the right. Just past that is a narrow asphalt road that leads up to the parking lot.

From I-77 North, take the Ripley exit and follow Rt. 33 East into Spencer. Go right on Rt. 119. Go through Spencer, and take a left on Rt. 36.

Length: 8.7 miles up to 12 miles, depending on your route.
Degree of Difficulty: ****
Scenery: ****
Topo Quads: Spencer and Looneyville.
Elevation (in feet): From 750 in the parking lot to about 1,100 in several places.
Footnotes: The hills and length of this ride make it a four star, but it should be no problem for bikers with any experience on single track. The Charles Fork Nature Trail

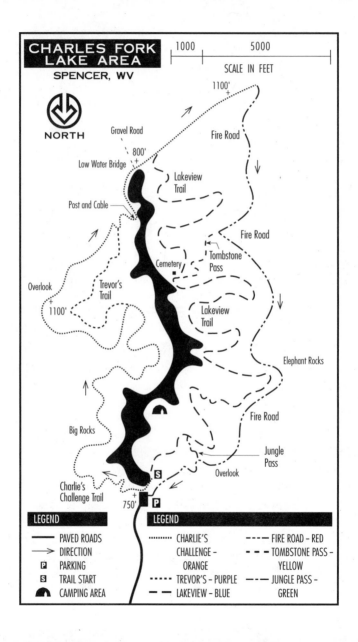

was built by bike-loving volunteers, with the help of a hard-working Boy Scout troop. The trail is fun, scenic, and physically challenging; i.e., it meets all the criteria for a good mountain bike ride. An additional 6 miles of trails were completed in early 1995, for a total of 15 miles of trails.

Description: By parking in the gravel lot near the dam, you can start and finish the trail in the same spot. It's up to you which end you start with, but I followed the trail sign and began by biking across the dam and into the woods. To start with the other end, simply head up the trail that goes uphill off the right side of the parking lot. It is marked by a cable between two posts.

Charlie's Challenge Trail goes across the dam and gently up into the woods. It loosely follows the contour of the lake, although you seldom see water. Pumping gradually uphill gets you to a fun series of roller coaster dips and turns, all punctuated by rocks and roots that give you a sense of never quite having your balance. Quick, small uphills greet you just as you think you can pick up some speed. Take a periodic break to get a glimpse of the critters you can hear rustling in the leaves. At one point I stirred up a hen turkey and her chicks, who scattered to hide in nearby limbs. I waited and watched as the chicks, one by one, fluttered out of the dense greenery and rejoined their mother on the forest floor.

At about 2.2 miles or so, Charlie's Challenge Trail intersects with Trevor's Trail. I went left and stayed on Charlie's Challenge, although Trevor's Trail is a little shorter route that ends up back on Charlie's Challenge. At 2.9 miles, you'll notice a clearing to the left, with a view of a valley dotted with farms. Stacks of blue mountains can be seen off in the distance, while cows graze the cleared hills in the foreground. The trail follows the perimeter of a farm for a while, offering other views of the Roane County countryside.

At 3.9 miles, you come to what looks like an intersection. Stay with the main trail to the right, where you begin a great series of drops that takes you to a dirt road near the lake. At 4.2 miles, there is a sharp left, then a sharp cut to the right at almost 4.3 miles. As you approach the road at 4.4 miles, a cable is stretched between two posts, cutting the trail. Since this is at the bottom of a downhill, watch your speed to avoid getting collared by the cable.

After you scoot under the cable, go left on the dirt road for a short distance. Turn right at 4.6 miles on a rutted road that goes through a pasture. From here you have two options: an easier ride on the Fire Road back, or more challenging single track on Lakeview Trail.

To access Lakeview Trail, turn right at about .1 mile into the rutted road. Lakeview itself meanders about 6 miles back to the starting point. At around 6.4 miles into the ride is a fork. Tombstone Pass goes off to the left and connects with the Fire Road. However, to stay on Lakeview, go right past a cemetery. At 9.8 miles on the left is Jungle Pass, which leads to the Fire Road. Stay right at 9.8 miles on Lakeview to reach the dam at 10.6 miles.

If you'd prefer to ride old road instead of single track, take the Fire Road. Back at 4.7 miles, go left (straight) on the rutted road instead of turning right onto Lakeview Trail. At 4.9 miles is a long climb. By keeping right, you will reach the Fire Road. The Fire Road rambles for several miles and eventually takes you back to the parking lot. At about 6.5 miles, Tombstone Pass goes off to the right to meet Lakeview Trail. Keep left on the Fire Road. At approximately 8.2 miles, Jungle Pass appears on the right. Stay left to travel down to the dam and your car. Watch out for the cable between the posts at the end of the trail. The latter route is a total ride of about 8.7 miles.

MORE RIDING IN THE AREA:

There are lots of back roads and service roads in the Spencer area that offer excellent riding. For suggested routes, contact the Roane County Chamber of Commerce at: P.O. Box 1, Spencer, WV 25276, (304) 927-4338. The Chamber of Commerce can also fill you in on the *Spencer Tour De Lake Mountain Bike Race* held each July.

WHERE TO STAY:

Camping and Lodging: Primitive camping is available at Charles Fork Lake. There is also hiking, fishing, and canoeing. Two miles west of Spencer on Rt. 33 is the Grandview Motel (304) 927-1840.

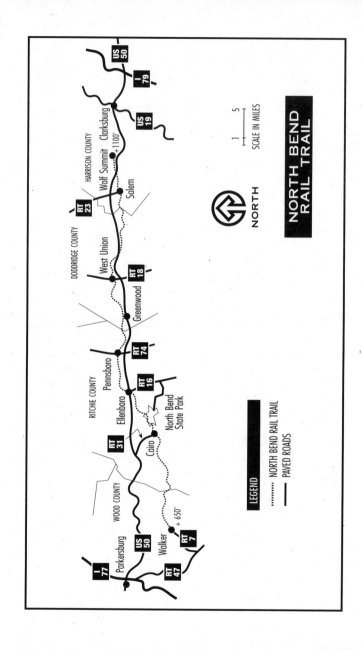

NORTH BEND
RAIL TRAIL

LEGEND

········· NORTH BEND RAIL TRAIL
———— PAVED ROADS

NORTH

|————|————|
1   5
SCALE IN MILES

16. NORTH BEND RAIL TRAIL

The North Bend Rail Trail follows the old Baltimore & Ohio Railroad main line from Walker, near Parkersburg, and travels east to Wolf Summit, near Clarksburg. The trail is part of the American Discovery Trail, which eventually will link the country from coast to coast. While model sections of the trail are generally in good condition and make for excellent riding, some areas are still not fully developed. The North Bend Rails to Trails Foundation Inc., along with the state, are dedicated to improving and upgrading the trail.

Along virtually any section of the North Bend trail you get a glimpse of the history of the area. The railroad culture is etched into these small towns and tunnels carved out of the rock. Area towns first revolved around the railroads; later it was the oil and gas industries. In Ellenboro, the glass industry is still thriving; you can even watch it in progress from the trail. A series of ovens, appearing like large, fire-breathing caskets, surround a small building. Glass fragments enter the ovens, and pellets exit. Other towns along the way have their roots in cigar manufacturing, the timber industry, and marble production.

Location: Wood, Ritchie, Doddridge and Harrison counties.
Directions: To access the trail from the western end in

Walker, take I-77 to Parkersburg. Then take Rt. 47 East for 7 miles to Rt. 7. Go left on Rt. 7; next go 4 miles to Walker. To access from the eastern end, take I-79 to Clarksburg. Take U.S. 50 West to the Wolf Summit exit.
Length: 61 miles.
Degree of Difficulty: *
Scenery: *** to ****
Topo Quads: not needed.
Elevations (in feet): Walker, 650; Wolf Summit, 1,100.
Footnotes: Difficulty rating is based on biking the trail in sections, rather than in one complete trip. The quality of the trail varies from wide, hard-packed gravel passages to nearly impassable, pocked stretches. The scenery varies as the old rail grade passes through woods, pastures, and small towns.

Description: The trail has a number of major access points, mainly along U.S. 50 as it runs between Parkersburg and Clarksburg. Following is a summary of access points, from west to east, as outlined by the North Bend Rails to Trails Foundation.

Walker - Exit Rt. 47 at Walker Rd.; go to where the road meets the trail at a barricade on the left.
Cairo - Take a right off U.S. 50 onto Rt. 31 and drive into Cairo.
Ellenboro - Exit U.S. 50 and take Rt. 16 for .25 mile to the trail.
Pennsboro - Exit U.S. 50 onto Rt. 74 into Pennsboro.
Greenwood - Take the Greenwood exit off U.S. 50 and catch the trail behind the State Division of Highways garage.

West Union - Exit U.S. 50 onto Rt. 18 to West Union.
Salem - Exit U.S. 50. Take Rt. 23 to Salem.

I have not traveled the entire North Bend Trail, but am familiar with sections east and west of Cairo on through Ellenboro and Pennsboro. These sections offer easy, interesting riding. The Cairo-to-Cornwallis-to-Ellenboro section is about 7 miles long, taking you through four tunnels. Picnic tables are available at points where the trail is adjacent to North Bend State Park. You will find a number of spots where you can stop to examine geologic features, historical points of interest, and the beautiful countryside. A good trip is an out-and-back from Cairo to Ellenboro, for a total of just under 14 miles. For a longer ride, continue on to Pennsboro, which adds 10 miles to the round trip.

For updated information on the condition of the trail, call the State Division of Tourism, or North Bend State Park at (304) 643-2931. An informative guide for the Ritchie County section of the trail was written in 1994 by Rock Wilson and Dean Six. To receive a guide, send $2.75 to: Berdine's 5 & Dime, 106 N. Court Street, Harrisville, WV 26362. It's a bargain, and has information on virtually every mile of the Ritchie County trail section. As a bonus, it contains rich detail on local history, from the story of the Silver Run Ghost to an account of the oil boom days of Cairo.

WHERE TO STAY:

Camping: North Bend State Park has a campground as well as cottages and a lodge for rent. For reservations call 1-800-CALL-WVA.

Bed & Breakfasts and Inns: Harmony House B&B (304) 485-1458 and The Blennerhasset Hotel (304) 422-3131 in Parkersburg; The Bias Farm (304) 643-4517 in Harrisville. Plenty of lodging is available in Parkersburg and Clarksburg.

MOUNTAINEER
COUNTRY

17. COOPERS ROCK
STATE FOREST

The highlight of this area for the sightseer is a rock overlook of the Cheat River Gorge. However, the highlight for the mountain biker is the 40 mile network of trails that weaves through the Coopers Rock Recreation Area and the adjacent West Virginia University Forest. All trails are open to hikers and bikers alike, year around. Within the recreation area are picnic sites and a campground for tents and trailers. Swimming and boating are available at nearby Cheat Lake. The forest has a trout pond open for fishing.

Within the recreation area is the Henry Clay Iron Furnace, a remnant of the early history of the area. The furnace, a 30-foot structure made of stone blocks, was part of the Cheat Mountain iron industry that flourished throughout much of the last century. About 200 men worked the furnace, which was at the center of a community of about 100 log houses, a church, school, and company store. The furnace is the only remaining evidence of the iron-making that took place here until 1847. The trail described below takes you past the furnace.

Directions: Coopers Rock State Forest is off I-68 about 11 miles east of Morgantown.

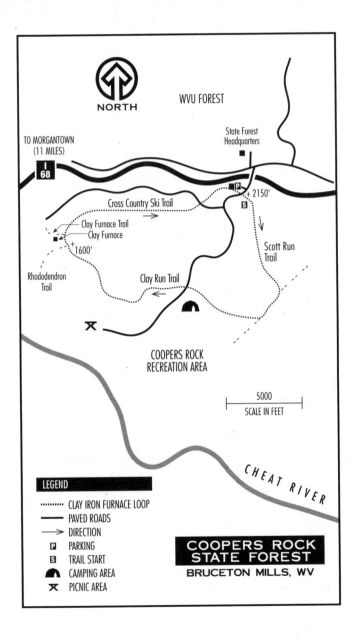

HENRY CLAY IRON FURNACE LOOP:

Location: Monongalia and Preston Counties.
Length: 7 mile loop.
Degree of Difficulty: ***
Scenery: ****
Topo Quads: Lake Lynn and Bruceton Mills.
Elevations (in feet): Between 1,600 and 2,200.
Footnotes: Difficulty rating is based on length, rocky surface of trails, and moderate climbs. You can shorten or lengthen this loop by dropping or adding trails. I chose a loop that wasn't too demanding and that would take me past the Henry Clay Iron Furnace. This loop gives access to a number of other trails in the area. By taking a left after exiting I-68 East, you can find the forest headquarters and get a trail map and advice on the current trail conditions.

Description: To start the loop, I parked at the entrance to the recreation area, which is on the right at Exit 15 East. Scott Run Trail starts into the woods on the left side of the road across from the parking lot. The day I rode I found about an inch of snow beautifully blanketing the forest. Initially, Scott Run Trail gently dips and turns across several small streams, most of which have bridges. At 1.8 miles into the trail, you cross several streams and the trail gets rocky. At 1.9 miles is an intersection. Go right up a moderate but rocky hill for .3 mile.

Underground springs enter the trail in several spots, making ice in the winter and mud in warmer weather. The ice is especially dangerous if you begin the trail from the other end and try to bike down the hill. Be cautious when biking downhill in snow, because it might be covering a slick patch of ice that will send you flying. At 2.8 miles, cross the paved road near the entrance to the camping area. From here, you can go right and bike along the road back to the park entrance, or catch Clay Run Trail. Clay Run Trail begins across the paved road past the campground. The trail passes a small pond, and then has a nice downhill ride of about 1.3 miles. Several optional trails branch off, but to reach the Clay Furnace stay on the main trail and follow the blue blazes. At about 4.7 miles from the start of Scott Run, you reach the Clay Furnace on the left.

From here, you can take Clay Furnace Trail for about 1 mile, then go right on a paved road that will take you back to the park entrance. You can also continue on the Clay Run Trail for a short distance to the park boundary. Or, you can catch the Rhododendron Trail and head to the picnic area and the rock overlook. Lastly, you can do what I did — take the Cross Country Ski Trail marked by a red blaze on the right, just up from the Clay Furnace Trail. The Cross Country Trail didn't have a painted marking when I rode it, but it essentially cuts along a hillside just past the Right Fork Creek. The trail is a gradual climb, with patches of rocks and roots. At about 6.5 miles, you reach a paved road. Pick up the trail on the other side. The trail enters a small meadow, then re-enters the woods to the right of the power line clearing. This stretch will take you back to the parking lot where you started, for a total ride of about 7 miles.

WHERE TO STAY:

Camping: The Forest has a 24 site camping area, picnic areas, and a bathhouse. Hunting and fishing are permitted with proper licenses. Call the Forest (304) 594-1561, or 1-800-CALL-WVA for more information.

Bed & Breakfasts and Inns: The following are in the Kingwood area: Inn Bed & Breakfast (304) 329-2793; Preston County Inn (304) 329-2220; and Victoria (304) 478-1103. Food and lodging are also available at the Heldreth Motel & Restaurant (304) 329-1145.

APPENDICES

I. Touring Companies

II. State Racing Information

III. Bicycle Clubs, Associations & Organizations

IV. Bicycle Shops

V. National Park and Forest Offices

VI. WV Average Temperatures & Precipitation

Appendix I

Touring Companies

Elk River Touring Center
Slaty Fork, WV 26291
(304) 572-3771

Ridge Rider Mountain Bikes
103 Keller Avenue
Fayetteville, WV 25840
(304) 574-2453

Elkins Bikeworks
218 Randolph Avenue
Elkins, WV 26241
(304) 636-9670

High Country Connections
HC 61, Box 156
Cass, WV 24927

Blackwater Bikes
P. O. Box 91
Davis, WV 26260
(304) 259-5286

Snowshoe Mountain Bike Center
P. O. Box 10
Snowshoe, WV 26209
(304) 572-1000

A.C.E. Whitewater
P. O. Box 1186
Oak Hill, WV 25901
(304) 469-2651

Free Spirit Adventures & Bike Shop
104 Foster Street
Lewisburg, WV 24901
(304) 645-2093

Pedals & Paddles Bike Shop
1100 Murdoch Avenue
Parkersburg, WV 26101
(304) 422-2453

**Greenbrier River
  Learning Center**
P. O. Box 160
Bartow, WV 24920
(304) 456-5191

Country Trails
P. O. Box 182
Cairo, WV 26337
(304) 628-3100

**Country Road
  Bike Rides**
P.O. Box 1470
Sheperdstown, WV
25443

WV Outdoor Adventures at The Greenbrier
White Sulphur Springs, WV 24986

Appendix II

State Racing Information

The West Virginia Mountain Bike Association (WVMBA) was formed in 1988. The purpose of WVMBA is to promote tourism and the interests of mountain bikers in West Virginia. WVMBA lobbies for multi-use trail access through political channels. WVMBA and the National Forest Service are partners for trail maintenance. WVMBA also promotes membership and sanctioned mountain bike racing. You can join the WVMBA at racing events for $12.00 annual dues. Contact the WVMBA at 774 Weaver Street, Morgantown, WV 26505, (304) 296-4142.

Following is a list of the WVMBA Racing Events:

Spring Challenge - April
Babcock State Park
Ridgeriders (304) 574-2453

Beander's MTB Rampage* - April
Elkins, WV (304) 636-9670

Challenge at Mountwood - May
Waverly, WV (304) 679-3611

Cannan Mountain Series #1 - May
Davis, WV (304) 259-5286

24 Hours of Canaan - June
Davis, WV (304) 259-5533

WV Fat Tire Festival* - June
Slatyfork, WV (304) 572-3771

Canaan Mountain Series #2* - July
Davis, WV (304) 259-5286

Tour de Lake* - July
Spencer, WV (304) 927-4338

Bunners Ridge* - July
Morgantown, WV (304) 291-2270

Black Bear 40K* - August
Kanawha State Forest
Charleston, WV (304) 925-8348

Snowshoe* - August
Snowshoe, WV (304) 572-1000

Knarly North Fork* - August
North Bend, WV (304) 259-5286

Whisper Twister* - August
Weston, WV (304) 452-8847

BOPARC "Go Fast If You Are" - August
Morgantown, WV (304) 291-2270

Henry Clay 30K* - September
Coopers Rock State Park
Morgantown, WV (304) 296-4142

Canaan Mountain Series #3 - September
Davis, WV (304) 259-5286

Fall Foliage 40K - September
Slatyfork, WV (304) 572-3771

Babcock Fall Challenge* - October
Babcock State Park (304) 574-2453

* Denotes WVMBA Point Series

APPENDIX III

WEST VIRGINIA BICYCLE CLUBS, ASSOCIATIONS & ORGANIZATIONS

North Bend Rails to Trails Foundation
c/o Kent Spellman
P.O. Box 206
Cairo, WV 26337
(304) 643-2618 W

Bicycle West Virginia, Inc.
c/o Greg Cook
2101 Washington St., East
Charleston, WV 25305
1-800-CALL-WVA

Charleston Recreational Bicycling Task Force
c/o Paul Wright
1510 Lewis Street
Charleston, WV 25311

Elk River Rails to Trails Foundation
c/o Randy Allio
P.O. Box 5556
Charleston, WV 25305
(304) 344-1885

Jaugstafl
c/o James Willis
Charleston, WV
(304) 744-7467 H

Mountain State Wheelers
c/o Dennis Strawn
P.O. Box 8161
South Charleston, WV 25303
(304) 347-7703

Vandalia Velos
c/o Craig Slaughter
P.O. Box 75145
Charleston, WV 25375
(304) 341-0701 W
(304) 345-9121 H

West Virginia Rails to Trails Council
c/o Frank Proud
P.O. Box 85
Nitro, WV 25143
(304) 722-6558

Harrison County Bicycle Association
c/o Bill Foster
515 South Linden Avenue
Clarksburg, WV 26301
(304) 624-9298 W

Gear Pushers
c/o Dan Ross
Route 1, Box 346-A
Fairmont, WV 26554
(304) 534-3959 H

New River Mountain Bike Club
c/o Mark Ashley
103 Keller Avenue
Fayetteville, WV 25480
(304) 574-453

Tri-State Wheelers Bicycle Club
c/o Karen Henline
590 Mahan Lane
Follansbee, WV 26037
(304) 527-1154

Greenbrier Valley Bike Club
c/o Al Youmans
Route 4, Box 77J
Frankfurt, WV 24938
(304) 497-2297 W
(304) 645-3220 H

**West Virginia Mountain Bike Association
(W.V.M.B.A.)**
c/o Jon Leyton
774 Weaver Street
Morgantown, WV 26505
(304) 296-4142

West Virginia Mojo's
c/o Laurie Schiffbauer
Morgantown, WV 26505
(304) 292-9000 W
(304) 292-2956 H

Blennerhasset Bicycle Club
c/o John Pellegrin
P.O. Box 2262
Parkersburg, WV 26102
(304) 429-2790 H

Mountain State Road Series
c/o Mike Holt
18 Dayton Road
Philippi, WV 26416
(304) 457-6230 W
(304) 457-2616 H

**Panhandle Alternative Transportation Alliance
(PAT Alliance)**
c/o Ms. Brandy Larrimore
Route 1, Box 755
Shepherdstown, WV 25443
(304) 876-3914

Shepherdstown Trail Committee
c/o David Malakoff
P.O. Box 727
Shepherdstown, WV 25443

Greenbrier River Trail Association
Gil Willis, President
General Delivery
Slatyfork, WV 26291
(304) 572-3771

APPENDIX IV

WEST VIRGINIA BICYCLE SHOPS

The Bicycle Store
112 Marshall Avenue
Beckley, WV 25801
(304) 253-5202

Backwoods Bike Shop
2009 Stadium Drive
Bluefield, WV 24701
(304) 327-5797

Country Trails
P. O. Box 352
Cairo, WV 26337
(304) 628-3100

Charleston Bicycle Center
409 53rd Street
Charleston, WV 25304
(304) 925-8348

John's Cyclery
309 MacCorkle Avenue
St. Albans, WV 25177
(304) 727-2180

High Country Bikes
489 1/2 N. Vance Dr.
Beckley, WV 25801
(304)255-2453

R & J Cycles
Racoon Run
Bristol, WV 26332
(304) 782-1144

**High Country
   Connection**
HC 61, Box 156
Cass, WV 24927

Mountain State Bicycles
107 Liberty Square
Hurricane, WV 25526
(304) 757-0308

Kid Country
908 Walnut Road
Charleston, WV 25314
(304) 342-8697

Rad Dag's California Connection
503 MacCorkle Ave., S.W.
South Charleston, WV 25303
(304) 768-7949

Curry's Bike Shop
107 21st Street
Nitro, WV 25143
(304) 755-8794

Blackwater Bikes
P. O. Box 91
Davis, WV 26260
(304) 259-5286

R.J. Bike and Ski Shop
1260 Hillcrest Road
Fairmont, WV 26554
(304) 574-2453

Huntington Bicycle Center
623 16th Street
Huntington, WV 25701
(304) 525-5312

South Hills Ski & Bike
364 MacCorkle Ave., S.E.
Charleston, WV 25304
(304) 345-3728

Holy Moses Bike Shop
645 West Pike Street
Clarksburg, WV 26301
(304) 622-7235

Elkins Bike Works
P.O. Box 129
Elkins, WV 26241
(304) 636-9670

Ridge Riders Mountain Bikes
103 Keller Avenue
Fayetteville, WV 25840

Jeff's Bike Shop
901 3rd Avenue
Huntington, WV 25701
(304) 522-2453

**Freespirit Adventures
  & Bike Shop**
104 Foster Street
Lewisburg, WV 24901
(304) 645-2093

**High Schwinn Cycle
  & Fitness**
279 Berkeley Plaza
Martinsburg, WV 25401
(304) 267-0816

The Pathfinder
235 High Street
Morgantown, WV 26505
(304) 296-0076

Whitetail Bikes
206 High Street
Morgantown, WV 26505
(304) 291-2270

Pedals & Paddles Bike Shop
1100 Murdoch Avenue
Parkersburg, WV 26101
(304) 422-2453

High Country Bikes
219 East Washington St.
Lewisburg, WV 24901
(304) 645-5200

Booth Cycles
202 Winchester Avenue
Martinsburg, WV 25401
(304) 263-5642

Wamsley Cycles
345 Spruce Street
Morgantown, WV 26505
(304) 296-2447

Bob's Bike Shop
2207 Camden Avenue
Parkersburg, WV 26101
(304) 424-6317

Saulville Bicycle Repair
Box 573
Pineville, WV 24874

Jack Horner's Corner
HC 64, Box 521
Seebert, WV 24946
(304) 653-4515

Elk River Touring Center
Slatyfork, WV 26291
(304) 572-3771

**Silver Creek Resort
  Mountain Bikes**
P. O. Box 83
Snowshoe, WV 26291
(304) 572-4000

**Snowshoe Mountain
  Biking Center**
P.O. Box 10
Snowshoe, WV 26209
(304) 572-1000

Vienna Bike Shop
2910 Grand Central Avenue
Vienna, WV 26105
(304) 295-5469

Wheelcraft Bicycles
107 Dallas Pike
Wheeling, WV 26059
(304) 547-0202

APPENDIX V

NATIONAL PARK AND FOREST OFFICES

Monongahela National Forest Headquarters
200 Sycamore Street
Elkins, WV 26241
(304) 636-1800

Cheat Ranger District
P.O. Box 368
Parsons, WV 26287
(304) 478-3251

Gauley Ranger District
Box 110
Richwood, WV 26261
(304) 846-2695

Greenbrier Ranger District
Box 67
Bartow, WV 24920
(304) 456-3335

Marlinton Ranger District
P.O. Box 210
Marlinton, WV 24954-0210
(304) 779-4334

Potomac Ranger District
HC 59, Box 240
Petersburg, WV 26847
(304) 257-4488

**White Sulphur Springs
  Ranger District**
410 East Main St.
White Sulphur Springs, WV
24986
(304) 536-2144

**Seneca Rocks
  Visitor's Center**
(304) 567-2827

**Cranberry Mountain
  Visitor's Center**
USDA Forest Service
P.O. Box 110
Richwood, WV 26261
(304) 653-4826

**New River Gorge
  National River**
246 Main Street
Glen Jean, WV 25846
(304) 465-0508

Appendix VI

West Virginia Average Monthly Temperatures & Precipitation

City		Jan.	Feb.	March	April	May	June	July	Aug.	Sept.	Oct.	Nov.	Dec.	Annual
Beckley	°F	29.2	32.1	42.0	51.2	59.5	66.2	69.7	68.8	62.8	52.4	43.4	34.0	50.9
	In.	2.92	2.94	3.40	3.43	3.98	3.84	4.70	3.38	3.33	2.89	2.99	3.23	41.03
Canaan Valley	°F	25.1	27.6	36.7	45.7	55.1	61.8	65.3	64.1	58.4	48.2	39.0	29.5	46.4
	In.	4.11	3.72	4.57	4.32	4.90	4.85	4.91	4.50	3.94	3.71	4.21	4.19	51.93
Charleston	°F	32.1	35.5	45.9	54.8	63.5	71.4	75.1	73.9	67.7	56.2	46.8	37.0	55.0
	In.	2.91	3.04	3.63	3.31	3.94	3.59	4.99	4.01	3.24	2.89	3.59	3.39	42.53
Elkins	°F	27.1	29.8	39.6	48.2	57.4	64.8	68.7	67.8	61.8	50.4	41.3	32.0	49.1
	In.	3.08	3.00	3.83	3.82	4.12	4.46	4.53	4.35	3.76	3.08	3.33	3.48	44.84

Lewisburg	°F	28.1	31.3	40.9	50.0	59.7	67.1	70.9	69.6	63.5	52.4	42.2	33.0	**50.7**
	In.	2.69	2.82	3.25	3.29	3.60	3.39	4.39	3.56	2.85	3.12	2.94	2.91	**38.81**
Morgantown	°F	29.0	31.8	42.3	51.8	61.4	69.1	72.9	71.7	65.4	54.1	44.4	34.3	**52.4**
	In.	2.51	2.48	3.75	3.48	3.95	4.04	4.27	4.01	3.52	2.74	3.27	3.19	**41.21**
Parkersburg	°F	29.9	33.0	43.9	53.3	62.7	70.6	74.4	73.2	66.8	55.3	45.4	35.1	**53.6**
	In.	2.59	2.74	3.87	3.60	3.91	3.67	4.26	4.16	3.19	3.03	3.28	3.21	**41.51**
Pickens	°F	27.0	29.8	39.4	48.2	57.0	63.9	67.2	66.2	60.8	50.7	41.1	31.7	**48.6**
	In.	4.80	4.55	5.72	5.52	5.74	5.47	6.52	5.68	4.90	4.59	5.14	5.38	**64.01**
Richwood	°F	30.1	32.7	42.3	51.0	59.3	65.8	69.5	68.4	62.6	52.2	43.2	33.3	**50.9**
	In.	3.26	3.31	4.05	4.15	4.64	4.30	5.53	4.78	3.55	3.71	3.72	3.84	**48.84**
Spencer	°F	29.2	32.4	42.6	52.3	61.6	69.2	73.1	71.7	65.4	53.8	44.2	34.3	**52.5**
	In.	3.03	2.89	3.63	3.58	3.89	3.44	4.83	4.16	3.60	3.23	3.55	3.36	**43.19**

About The Author

My romance with rural West Virginia started soon after I arrived in Charleston as a reporter for the *Charleston Daily Mail*. I grew up on a farm in Kentucky. As a result, I have found that I need regular doses of the countryside. Fortunately, my job allowed me to travel across West Virginia and experience not only its natural beauty, but also the character of its people. As a journalist, I was allowed to explore the state and become familiar with some of its most precious sights. Mountain biking seemed a natural way to get to know the Mountain State on a more intimate basis. I am not an expert biker, but rather one who loves to bike and write. Thus the book. I began riding and taking notes on trails in the spring of 1994, and continued through that summer. My travels as a reporter helped a great deal as I searched for interesting places to ride. I hope this book reflects the passion I feel for the West Virginia countryside.

I left Charleston in August of 1994 to begin graduate work in Wisconsin. I would like nothing more than to return to West Virginia to write a second volume of mountain biking trails. If you have suggestions for new trails, or remarks on this book, I'd love to hear from you. Write to me care of: Trans Allegheny Books, 118 Capitol Street, Charleston, WV 25301.

PHOTO CREDITS

Cover, Tina Hall; p. 2, P. Broughton; p. 14, P. Broughton; p. 18, F. Hutchins; p. 27, Lisa Marshall, courtesy of Paul and Robin Broughton; p. 30, F. Hutchins; p. 47, Neal Palumbo-Singletrack Photography, courtesy of Laird Knight; p. 52, P. Broughton; p. 62, P. Broughton; p. 72, F. Hutchins; p. 80, Tina Hall, courtesy of P. and R. Broughton; p. 90, F. Hutchins; p. 98, P. Broughton; p. 106, P. Broughton; p. 112, P. Broughton; p. 114, P. Broughton; p. 123, L. Marshall, courtesy of P. and R. Broughton; p. 128, P. Broughton; p. 134, L. Marshall, courtesy of P. and R. Broughton; p. 142, T. Hall, courtesy of P. and R. Broughton; p. 148, T. Hall, courtesy of P. and R. Broughton; p. 154, L. Marshall, courtesy of P. and R. Broughton; p. 166, P. Broughton; Back cover, T. Hindman.